Playing Computer
Chess

Getting the Most Out of Your Game

Al Lawrence
& Lev Alburt

Sterling Publishing Co., Inc.
New York

To my wife, Daphne, who makes everything
not only possible but fun, and to Samson,
who sat with me through every word.
              —Al Lawrence

Acknowledgments and Credits
The authors would like to thank the following for their help and support,
which made this book possible: Gary Colvin, Fairfield Hoban, Alan Kantor,
Kent Nelson, Judy Shipman, and Helen Warren.

For graphics: Don Addis, p. 129; Nick Alfonso, pp. 50, 58; ChessBase, p.
38 (Fritz); Chess Cafe, p. 135; Kevin Dyke, pp. 6, 62, 112, 113; Excalibur, on
cover (Squire); Internet Chess Club, p. 136; Interplay, p. 4 bottom (Battle
Chess), pp. 4 right, 81 (Chess Mates); Al Lawrence, p. 9 (2), 110, 121;
Mindscape, p. 4 (Database), 4 middle, 10 (ChessMaster); Konstantin Moshkin,
p. 14; Jillian Nelson, p. 125; Rich Rosales, p. 35; Heiser Zedonek, p. 71; all
other artwork (pp. 18, 28, 40, 41, 45, 83, 93, 108, 111, 124) Patricia Melvin.

Edited by Claire Bazinet

Library of Congress Cataloging-in-Publication Data Available

10 9 8 7 6 5 4 3 2

Published by Sterling Publishing Company, Inc.
387 Park Avenue South, New York, N.Y. 10016
© 1998 by Al Lawrence and Lev Alburt
Distributed in Canada by Sterling Publishing
℅ Canadian Manda Group, One Atlantic Avenue, Suite 105
Toronto, Ontario, Canada M6K 3E7
Distributed in Great Britain and Europe by Cassell PLC
Wellington House, 125 Strand, London WC2R 0BB, England
Distributed in Australia by Capricorn Link (Australia) Pty Ltd.
P.O. Box 6651, Baulkham Hills, Business Centre, NSW 2153, Australia
Manufactured in the United States of America
All rights reserved

Sterling ISBN 0-8069-0717-7

Contents

Introduction

This is a book with a mission and a plan. (Chess players learn quickly that the best results come from this approach.) It will show you how to beat your chess computer and, in the process, teach you how to play better chess against anyone—or anything!

Don't worry about whether you know all—or even any—chess rules. Included in the back of this book for reference is the U.S. Chess Federation's official summary. It explains all the moves clearly, and the rules are the same all over the world.

This book is about traditional chess—the only kind recognized by the World Chess Federation. Whenever the media talk about chess or the world chess championship, this is the "chess" they have in mind. Variants of this classic game (*Star Trek*'s 3D chess, for example) have never really caught on because of some problem with their rules or a lack of the logic, poetry and beauty of "real" chess.

Traditional chess seems to offer just the right balance of strategy and tactics to capture the human imagination. Like most appealing disciplines, like the laws of the physical universe itself, its discrete possibilities (the number of possible moves, for example) are nearly limitless, yet the governing principles can be reduced to a finite and very manageable number.

Inside these chapters, you'll see "snapshots," diagrams of games, along with explanations. They'll show you how to beat your own personal microchip chess monster, as well as human opponents. You will also discover how to find human chess opponents—for face-to-face, through-the-mail, or over-the-modem play. Nowadays you can play a chess opponent in Sweden, or in Singapore, with the same ease that you can tune in your favorite radio station. You'll also get the inside scoop on where computers and humans stand in the battle for chess supremacy—and we think you'll be surprised!

Along the way, you'll find out some amusing and amazing things about chess and the people who play. You'll discover that very few of them actually hold their spectacles together at the nose piece with white adhesive tape!

So relax. You're going to have fun! And you're going to learn to beat those micro-chip monsters!

Al Lawrence   International Grandmaster Lev Alburt

Chess is a game of understanding, not of memory.
—Znosko-Borovsky

CHAPTER ONE

Take a Break, Mister Spock. Chess Is a Human Game; That's Why Jim Always Beats You

You may already have a chess computer partner that has been bullying you—a tabletop model chess set with a fat board, a hand-held wizard, or a software program on your PC. Or you may have been invited to try a friend's and been soundly defeated. Maybe you've just heard that computers trounce humans at chess—that computers are *unbeatable* at chess.

It simply isn't so. Humans can still play chess better than computers.

Despite what you may have seen on the evening news about IBM's computer, called "Deeper Blue" in its 1997 incarnation, few insiders believe that computers yet rule the world of chess. Many believe that computers may *never* be supreme. We'll get to the specifics of this idea later, but for now, understand that these nay-sayers are not sour-grape computer bashers. They have legitimate reasons—grounded both in solid computer science and the fundamentals of chess—for their belief.

Recall those classic, original *Star Trek* episodes in which Mr. Spock, the half-Vulcan with the computerlike brain, *always* lost to his emotional and inspiration-driven Captain Kirk. Though their game of choice was a flawed version of traditional chess called "3D" chess, the plot line was foresightedly correct. The scriptwriters understood something about humans versus computers—an opinion evidently shared with some modern experts. They believed that, in certain intellectual pursuits, computers would *never* rule.

But recent computer developments have put a rather surprising twist to this debate. Many defenders of our species felt that humans would remain in charge because of their capacity for surprising inspiration, and thus defeat chip-cold logic.

Humans can apply the logic of chess better than computers can!

Surprise! The truth is paradoxical. Humans beat computers because we mortals are better at applying logic! Any computer worth its silicon can analyze many more moves per second than a human. IBM's "Deeper Blue," which won its 1997 match against Professional Chess Association World Chess Champion Garry Kasparov, "saw" 200 million positions per second! Computers often find the poetic "surprises" because they look at so much. Indeed, even when they find these "beautiful" shots, the computers consider them just another move. Rest assured, there's no special place in the computer's component "heart" for the beautiful or surprising. But the real surprise is what computers *don't* do so well—effectively applying the *guiding principles* of winning chess to actual play. That's what human brains are better at!

There are special strategies that will help you beat your computer, and later chapters will point them out clearly. But in large part, learning to beat your chess computer is like learning to beat other humans. You'll learn some basic guiding principles that chess masters down through the centuries have discovered and distilled. And there are some tricks, like the "Rule of the Square," amounting to calculation aids, that allow you to amaze the uninitiated. You'll simply get better. And like the boxer in training, you'll use a punching bag before you have to go out and try your moves on other humans. Well, okay, the computers will punch back—but it can all be handled very privately!

Millions of chess computers and chess computer software programs have been sold. There's an incredible range of chess computers—from handheld models that sell for around $20 and run on triple-A batteries to the IBM twin-tower mainframe into which the multinational corporation has invested millions of dollars. It does take the grandmasters—the elite humans of the chess world—to handle computers on the top end. The rest of us can certainly be given a tough game by the commercially available stand-alone or software chess player.

Your chess computer will never turn down a game, knock the pieces over, or snicker at your bad moves

Actually, there are commercially available chess computers-with-attitudes programmed to belittle you. They'll even ask insulting questions. One, during a "friendly" game, asked me, in an unnervingly real-sounding voice, "Are you a salesman? Only a salesman would make a move like that!" But our sub-chapter heading is true. They'll never turn you down, and they'll never make a scene by being a bad loser—or winner.

You see, the truth is, the authors like computers–they're handy, do our bidding, ready to serve, day or night. We're using one now to write this book, and we *love* chess computers. They make strong practice partners available to everyone. Can't sleep and want to do something better than watch TV infomercials? Switch on your ever-ready electronic partner. The increased popularity of chess–one of those rare games that give you back something valuable for your time–owes much to chess computers.

Let's get to know our "friendly enemy"

Let's take a look at a few chess computers of the type that may challenge you. They're all available at electronics and other stores. You can find one in every big mall and through catalogs. Commercial chess computers are divided into *stand-alone chess computers* and *software programs* for your PC.

Stand-alone chess computers offer you the advantage of playing chess more or less as people have for centuries. You feel and move the pieces on an actual board. Normally, the board itself houses the microprocessor.

Stand-alone chess computers can be plastic-peg sets that fit in your palm or real-wood beauties that look great on your coffee table.

Software programs are normally very strong players without the big price tag of top-of-the-line stand-alones. But you need a personal computer to use them. Of course, a given program's strength varies based on the configuration of your PC. The more soup your home computer has, the better the software will perform.

Most home PC software offer all the features, are simple to use, and give you printing options. If you like using a mouse for play on a two-dimensional representation of a chessboard, they are fine. Of course, they don't travel well—except on a laptop.

The newest computers offer a legion of features. Some of these features—such as selectable levels of play, as well as "hint" and "move-take-back" options—make it a lot faster and easier to learn to play winning chess. Nearly all the models offer similar options. But there's a key feature that sometimes *isn't* offered.

One feature is sometimes missing—and it's crucial! Be sure to get a computer with a "set-up" option. This allows you to quickly set up any position you want to practice. The feature is an absolute "must" for getting the most out of your chess computer—and out of this book!

The good news is that, even if you already own a chess computer, it probably has the set-up option. And if it doesn't, the prices of these programmed partners are getting so low that you can afford to buy a new one that does offer set-up.

Without even being switched on, your computer can teach you how to read and write chess

So dust off that source of humiliation and take another look. If it's a stand-alone model, you don't even have to turn it on to learn a lot. Position it in front of you, so that its printing and labeling appears right-side up. Set the pieces aside for a moment. Let's take a close look at the top of the chessboard. If you have software, follow the directions to install it, if you haven't done this already. Boot it up on your program. You can quickly view an empty board by selecting the "clear board" option. For the sake of brevity, we'll refer only to the stand-alone models as we describe the board and pieces. The basics are the same for a software program.

Boards come in all sizes and several colors. But they all have eight rows of eight squares—64 in all—alternating in two colors or shades, usually light and dark. Chess players talk about *light* and *dark* squares. There are 32 of each. You'll notice that the right-hand corner square closest to you is light (probably white, gray, or silver-colored) rather than dark.

Despite all the dumb set-up mistakes made in magazine ads, TV commercials and movies, the board must always be positioned so that both opponents have a light square in the right-hand corner closest to them.

Each of the 64 squares has an "address" that's easy to remember once you know the basics of the simple grid invented by chess players to label the *files*—the eight up-and-down columns—and the *ranks*—the eight side-to-side rows. The files are designated by letters, *a* through *h*, from White's left to right. The ranks are numbered, *1* through *8*, again, from bottom to top from *White's* point of view. Here's an important convention: Whenever the chessboard is portrayed, White is at the bottom, moving "up." So let's take a look at an empty board labeled in the way that the one on your computer may be.

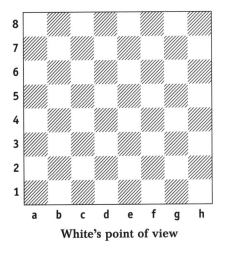

White's point of view

The chessboard can be understood as a series of eight up-and-down files, labeled *a–h*, and eight left-to-right ranks, labeled *1–8*.

Here it's easy to see what chess players mean when they talk about the "a-file." It's simply the up-and-down column of squares on White's far left. The "first rank" is the horizontal row of squares right under White's nose. These files and ranks make a grid, like the grid of streets and cross streets in a well-laid-out town. Each square on the grid is located at the intersection of a file and a rank—and it's known by that address. The square at White's near-left corner, for example, is called "a1."

Your computer could have letters and numbers that identify the ranks and files alongside, or it could have each square labeled like this. ▶

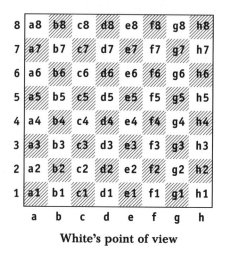

White's point of view

How your computer communicates with you

This book isn't an instructional manual for your computer; yours came with one. If you've lost it, that's no big deal either. Just call or write the company for a new set of instructions. One of three companies probably made your stand-alone chess computer if you bought it in the United States:

      Excalibur Electronics, Inc., Miami, Florida

      Saitek Industries, Ltd., Torrance, California

      Novag Industries, Ltd., Hong Kong

In our testing we used two major software-playing programs and a chess program: Battle Chess by Interplay (makers also of Chess Mates, animated instructional chess software for children, and the upcoming USCF Chess, Interplay's improved software); ChessMaster 5000, the strongest-playing and easiest to use of the popular software, by Mindscape; and "Fritz" by ChessBase (also makers of Chess-Base, a favorite of tournament players for the ease it gives to extracting specific information from hundreds of thousands of master games).

The most common way of making your move on stand-alone computers is to press down on the "from" and "to" squares with your piece. Then your computer has to tell you where to move its piece or pawn in response. Your computer may even have little red lights on each square. In this case, it will light up the "from" square, and when you press that square, it will light up the "to" square. Or your computer may have a Liquid Crystal Display (LCD) instead. This little window into your computer's mind will display the "from" and "to" squares to confirm your moves and to communicate its responses. It uses what chess players call "computer algebraic notation." It's a big phrase for a little idea. The computer just uses the addresses of the "from" and "to" squares with a little dash between them. Humans, when talking or writing to each other, prefer to use a little different variation. A few moves of an example game will show you the difference.

For example, you play **1. e2-e4**. The computer may display as its response **e7-e5**. Because these are both pawn moves, there is no difference between *computer algebraic* and regular *algebraic notation*.

> **Chess players give strong moves a "!" and weak moves a "?"**

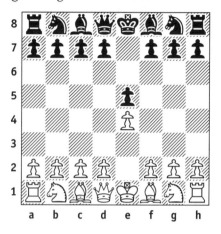

Here's the position. ▶

Of course, there are a lot of possible plays from here, but, just for the sake of the example, let's assume the game follows a familiar opening pattern called the Ruy López, named after a sixteenth-century Spanish clergyman who was the best player of his era and a favorite at the court of Philip II. Below, on the left, is *computer algebraic notation*, the square-to-square method, which you'll need to know to get along with your chess computer–after all, communication is the key to a good relationship. On the right is the human-preferred *algebraic notation*, which differs because, when a piece–not a pawn–is involved, the abbreviation of the piece name appears before the "from" square. Both notation systems are a cinch to learn. As you go along in this book, you will get plenty of practice. Just keep the difference between the two systems in mind.

2. g1-f3	b8-c6	2. Ng1-f3	Nb8-c6
3. f1-b5	a7-a6	3. Bf1-b5	a7-a6

Yet another form of this notation is *short algebraic*. It's just like the form on the right-hand column, except it leaves out the "from" square, and depends on the piece symbol alone to identify the piece that's moving, or in the case of a pawn, we simply write the "to" square. (When two like pieces can move to the same square, then we revert to the long form to avoid confusion.) The short form is used to save time. The first three moves of the Ruy López in short algebraic are 1. e4 e5 2. Nf3 Nc6 3. Bb5 a6. We'll use the long form throughout this book.

Diagonals

Besides ranks and files, chess players understand their board as a series of diagonals, two or more squares of like color connected at their corners. There are two diagonals that run from corner to corner, intersecting the center of the board. These are called the *long diagonals*. The *long diagonal* that runs from a1 to h8 is made up of dark squares. The *long diagonal* that runs from h1 to a8 is a light-square diagonal. There are 26 diagonals on the board, 13 light and 13 dark. The longer the diagonal, the more likely it is to be of strategic importance in a game.

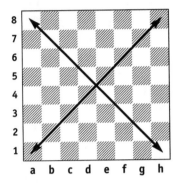

The long diagonals run from corner to corner, through the center.

So that's the nature of the battlefield and how to read the moves. Don't worry, we'll be reviewing all of this as we go along, using many diagrams.

You may knock your opponent down with the chessboard, but that does not prove that you are the better player.
—English proverb

"I said, we play by *my* rules!"

You can't depend on your eyes when
your imagination is out of focus.
—Mark Twain

CHAPTER TWO

Visualizing the Goal

If there's one thing that will make you superior to even very, very strong chess-playing computers, it's your human ability to *plan*–to understand a goal, to keep it in focus, and to visualize the steps that will move you toward that goal. (After all, chess both teaches and requires this basic key to success. People of all ages and backgrounds have given the game credit for literally changing their lives, making them more effective than they ever dreamed.) Keeping a long-term goal in mind is much different from visualizing a string of moves and "what-if" subvariations–computers do that process flawlessly. Their "brains" never get tired, their inner "eye" never gets foggy. But when they exhaust the room in their "search memory," they tend to just stop calculating. They count the pieces, make their evaluation, and make their decision–however exciting and risky the position.

In this way, chess computers keep running into their *horizon effect*, that is, they can ignore a critical point because they simply won't look far enough to see it. Human players in such a position can "sense" a big moment coming up and force themselves to look farther, or they simply aim toward a goal following their "intuition." Even with their unerring ability to "see" each future position within their horizons, computers aren't great long-range planners.

The *horizon effect* causes the computer to walk a plank into a swirling school of sharks because it is being chased with a fly swatter. It won't look far enough to see the danger at the end of the plank.

So, let's emphasize our human advantage. Let's have our ultimate goal clearly in mind from the beginning. Your goal in chess is to checkmate the King. Checkmate comes from the Persian words "shahk matt," meaning "the King is dead." Okay, that's the metaphor, but what does this actually mean on the board?

Checkmate means that the King is attacked by one or more pieces, and can't get out of check in the one move at a time each turn is entitled to.

It's a set-up!

It's time to get familiar with the "set-up mode" on your computer so that you can practice the basic positions in this book. This feature makes it possible for you to play against your computer in any legal position. Of course, your computer doesn't "see" the position you set up on the board until you push a few special buttons. Otherwise, your computer assumes that you're beginning a game with the pieces set up on their original squares), and "knows" how the position is changing with each move. To start from a special position, you need to tell it where the pieces are. Knowing how to do this makes your computer a lot more fun, and infinitely more instructive.

Even though there are a few chess computers that will talk to you, none at this writing will listen to your human voice. Button-pressing is the *Esperanto,* the common language. The words "set-up" or "setting-up problems" will probably appear in the Table of Contents in your computer's instruction booklet. Don't be intimidated. The process really is easy, and after you work through it a few times, it will be second nature. Here are the general steps most stand-alone computers require. Remember, look at the paragraph covering "set up" in your computer's manual to check the specifics—exactly what keys to press in what order.

✓Tell your computer you want to play a "new game." (There's often a key on the control panel clearly marked "new game.") This will clear the final position of the previous game from the computer's memory. On many chess computers, simply turning the unit off and on does not start a new game.

✓Enter "set-up mode" by pressing a key or two. (Usually a key marked "set-up.")

✓Clear the board. Since, in its "brain," your computer sets up all the pieces in their game-starting positions for a new game, these need to be erased. (Normally you will be required to press a different key once or even twice to clear the board.)

✓Set up the new position by identifying, one by one, the pieces you want to include and the squares you want each piece to stand on. This is normally done by pressing a "piece key" that shows a symbol of a specific piece, for example, ♔ for a King, and then pressing the square you want it located on. Be sure to get the right color by checking your computer's display. Normally you set the color correctly before identifying and locating the piece.

You'll be a champ at this after only a few of the diagrams coming up. Since our positions usually have only a few pieces in them, the set-up process will be quick and painless.

A word about models and playing levels

Throughout the book, we've used a variety of stand-alone models and software programs. We couldn't of course, use any that did not offer "set-up mode." We don't identify the specific model of the stand-alones for a number of reasons. This book isn't a commercial plug for any particular brand or model. Nor is it a comprehensive buying guide. We do let you know whether in a particular example we're using a basic ($20–$49), mid-range ($50–$79), or upscale ($80 and up) stand-alone chess computer. When a computer has been officially rated by the United States Chess Federation, we note that fact. We used two widely available and popular software programs—ChessMaster 5000 from Mindscape and Battle Chess from Interplay. We also used one specialty chess software program, "Fritz" from ChessBase USA. None of these are rated by USCF, but all are strong players, especially Fritz, which is well into the "Senior Master" class.

We played the computers on a number of "levels." You can play your computer without worrying about setting levels. The level the computer goes to automatically when you first put batteries in it, its "default level," is set so that a non-tournament player can get an opponent that will respond quickly. (The higher the level, the more "thinking" time the computer requires.) We'll let you know when we drastically changed levels. Certainly, if you begin to beat your computer consistently, you should advance its level so that you don't become bored. Changing levels is easy. Usually, you just press a "level" key. Check your instruction booklet.

Two basic mating situations

Here are two series of checkmates, our goal. The first are examples that illustrate winning as a result of having a big *material* advantage—owning more pieces than your opponent. You can then bully him into checkmate, the way a beefy professional wrestler could overpower a normal human and pin him to the canvas. The second series of checkmates illustrates the possibilities when material is equal, or even when the ultimate winner is behind in material. Here the player delivering mate uses superior strategy and tactics, the way a judo master might feint to catch even a huge and more muscular opponent off balance.

Wrestled to the mat by superior material

All these are the basic "forced mates." The superior side can always mate the other side. To see how the computers approach this task, and how the mates should be executed, USCF chess master Alan Kantor becomes our human gladiator. He takes the losing side and defends staunchly to test the computer's mettle. Sometimes he then takes the other side to see how well the computer defends. If you follow us through this process, you'll learn the basic mates, and you'll find some interesting chinks in the collective space-age plastic of computers!

Against a lone King defender, the minimal material needed to *force* mate is Rook and King. One Bishop and King or one Knight and King cannot force mate. There is one interesting exception: a King and two Knights cannot force mate against a lone King, even though normally two Knights are worth more than one Rook.

King and two Rooks vs. King

This is a very easy mate once you know the pattern. The King on the winning side does not even have to participate! It's faster for the long-range Rooks to do it all. *The method is to force the defending King to the edge of the board, where one Rook pens him in while the other Rook checks and mates him.*

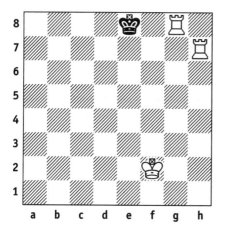

◀ Here's a "snapshot" of what the final mating position looks like.

Checkmate!
The White Rooks are so powerful in tandem that they don't require assistance from their King. Black is driven to the edge of the board, hemmed in and mated!

Here's the position we challenged the computer with. ▶

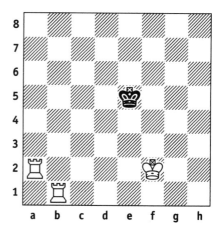

We tried a mid-range computer that has a USCF Expert's rating when set to tournament levels. We left it at its default level since this mate is so easy. But it couldn't mate! It gave up a draw after 36 moves, by three-time repetition—when the same position occurs three times, either player can claim a draw. We were surprised at this result!

So Alan turned the tables to demonstrate how it should be done. We boosted the computer's level of play to improve its defensive technique. Alan mates it in seven without much thought, because he keeps the goal clearly in mind.

Alan vs. mid-level (rated Expert)

1. Ra2-a4
Excellent, the very first move "builds a fence" to restrict the opposing King to a small rectangle.

1. ...   Ke5-d6
An error, conceding a whole rank before he had to. This shortens Black's resistance. Correct is 1. ... Ke5-d5. Of course, Black is lost anyway, but we see the computer failing to apply the basic logic of the position.

2. Rb1-b5   Kd6-c6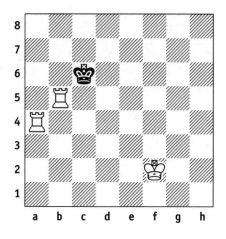

This attack on the Rook is the best move in the position. White has to take a move to re-deploy his Rook out of the King's reach.

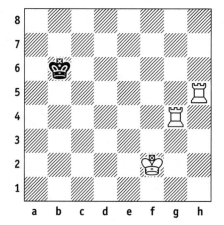

◄

3. Rb5-h5   Kc6-b6
4. Ra4-g4

Now White is ready to apply the "lawnmower technique": The Rooks mow down the board row by row.

4. ....   Kb6-c6
5. Rg4-g6+   Kc6-b7 ►

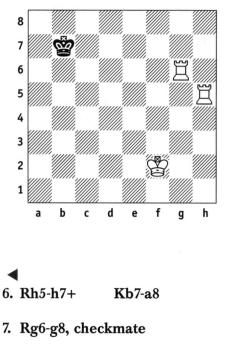

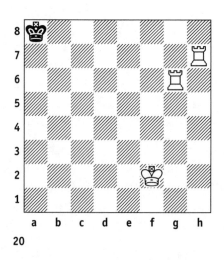

◄

6. Rh5-h7+   Kb7-a8

7. Rg6-g8, checkmate

King and Queen against King

This basic position can be won, with best play for both sides, in no more than 10 moves. But don't memorize moves! Just keep in mind the methods and the snapshot of the final position. *The basic method is to drive the opposing King to the edge of the board and mate him by using both your King and Queen.* Here's how the final position looks (it could be located anywhere on the edges of the board). ▶

Checkmate!
The defending King has been driven to the edge of the board, where the attacking Queen is supported by her King.

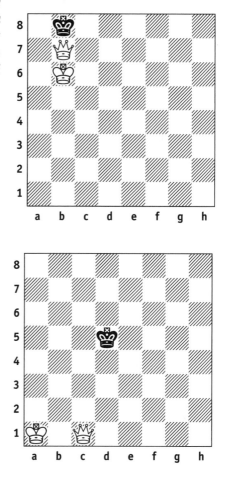

Here is the starting position we used for our test. ▶

The computer—a popular mid-range model with simulated "voice" and a vocabulary of bullying wise-cracks—could not mate Alan on its default level 6 (levels 1–5 are actually stronger "ply-search" levels on this model). It too fell into a draw by repeating the position three times on move 21! There's a message here: When you're playing against your computer, make it mate you. Maybe it can't!

No one has ever won a game by resigning.
  –Grandmaster Savielly Tartakover

Nor has anyone drawn a chess computer *by resigning!**
  –Alburt & Lawrence

*With sympathy for World Champion Garry Kasparov, who should have followed this advice in Game 2 against Deeper Blue in 1997 (see Chapter 5).

So we cranked our trash-talking computer up to level 16, about ten seconds per move. It showed us it could now force the mate, although it didn't do so in the fastest, most logical way. Let's take a look how, when he turned the tables again, Alan dispatched the computer.

Alan vs. mid-range (rated Expert)

1. Qc1-f4
Excellent! He cuts the defender off from half the board on move 1!

1. ...   Kd5-c5
Black tries to stay as close to the center for as long as possible, since he can be mated only on the edge of the board, where his mobility is reduced. Somewhat better would be to run to the side away from White's King, since the rival monarch will have to help with the checkmate. So already, the computer has made a mistake. Humans, visualizing the goal, would apply logic and move to e6.

2. Qf4-d2
Now Black is limited to just three rows!

2. ...   Kf5-c4
Black doesn't voluntarily give up another row.

3. Qd2-d6   Kc4-c3
See how Alan is forcing the computer's King toward his own, to shorten the process? ▼

4. Qd6-d5
Tightening up the box. Humans don't have to memorize these moves. They simply remember the logic.

4. ...   Kc3-b4

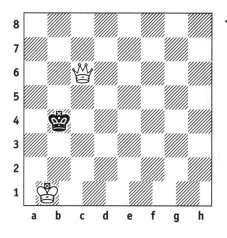

◀ **5. Qd5-c6**
Another row is cut off.

5. ...   **Kb4-b3**
6. Qc6-c5   **Kb3-a4**
There was no other move. Black has to acquiesce in moving to the very last row at his disposal. Now that he is on the edge, the end comes quickly.

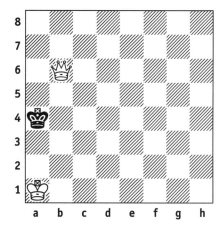

7. Qc5-b6   ▶

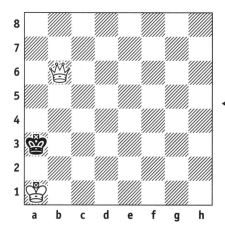

◀ **7. ...**   **Ka4-a3**
White has to stay awake here! Notice that 8. Qb3-b5 leaves Black with no moves, and NOT in check. Stalemate—a draw! But we'll avoid that, of course.

8. Ka1-b1   **Ka3-a4**
9. Kb1-c2   **Ka4-a3**
10. Qb6-b3 mate   ▶
A variation on our goal—but a very acceptable one!

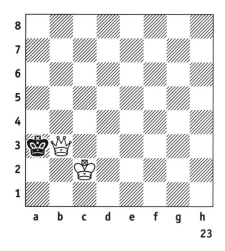

King and one Rook vs. King

A very practical mate to understand. With best play on both sides, this mate takes no more than 16 moves from any position. *The correct method is to force the defending King to the edge, and then to the corner of the board, forcing a position in which the other King pens him to the edge while the Rook checkmates.*

The final position looks like this. ▶

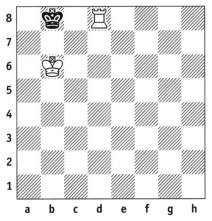

Checkmate!
Black's King must be driven to the edge of the board, hemmed in by the opposing King, and then attacked by the Rook.

We challenged a different mid-range stand-alone with the following position. We found that, at only four seconds per move, it found the mating procedure. But its play did not demonstrate the logic of the procedure very well. So we asked Alan to take the stronger side. ▼

Alan vs. mid-range

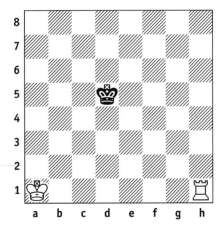

1. Rh1-h4
Once again building the first fence, cutting down the Black King's playground.

1. ...   Kd5-e5
2. Ka1-b2
White will need his King to help the Rook checkmate.

2. ...   **Ke5-d6**   ▶

Again, without the ability to understand White's goal, Black can't find the best defense, which is to stay away from the edge for as long as he can with 2. ... Ke5-d5! Of course, Black would still lose to best play, but he would make it as hard as possible for White.

3. Rh4-h5   **Kd6-e6**
4. Kb2-c3   **Ke6-d6**   ▼

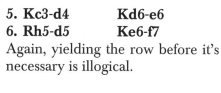

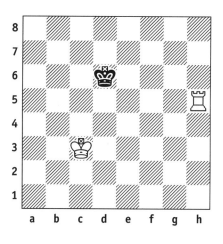

5. Kc3-d4   **Kd6-e6**
6. Rh5-d5   **Ke6-f7**
Again, yielding the row before it's necessary is illogical.

7. Kd4-e5   **Kf7-g6**
8. Ke5-f4   **Kg6-f7**
9. Rd5-e5   **Kf7-g7**

10. Kf4-g5   **Kg7-g8**   ▶

Our electronic pal just doesn't get it! Of course, Kg7-f7 is better. But Alan is relentlessly making the pen smaller and smaller, so the end is inevitable.

11. Re5-e7
Now the Black King is against the edge of the board. Mate will follow quickly.

11. ...   **Kg8-f8**

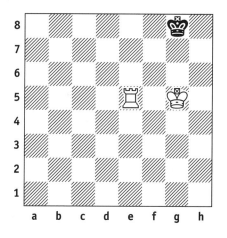

12. Kg5-f6   Kf8-g8

Take special note of the next maneuver. It's the key to the mating procedure once the defender is on the edge.

13. Re7-b7

A waiting move! Black's King can't move to f8 because Rb7-b8 would be checkmate.

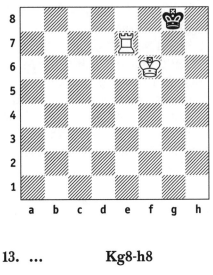

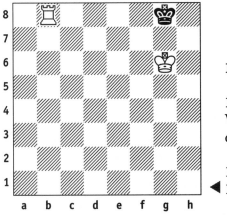

13. ...   Kg8-h8

14. Kf6-g6

White is forcing Black to "bounce off the wall" into checkmate.

14. ...   Kh8-g8

◀ **15. Rb7-b8 checkmate**

King and two Bishops vs. King

You won't run into this very often, perhaps never. It's relatively easy—though the computers didn't think so!—since the Bishops together can control both light and dark squares. We're not going to play out the ending here, but with best play it takes no more than 18 moves, even from the "worst" position for the attacking side. *The method is to drive the King into the corner.*

Here's a position showing one example of the mate. ▶

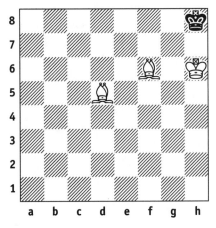

Checkmate!
With the two Bishops, the defending King has to be driven into the corner, where it is trapped and put in check.

We tested ChessMaster 5000 from this "worst case" position. ▶

We set the program on its problem-solving mode, running on a Pentium, 200 Megahertz processor—among the fastest PC configurations at the time of this writing. Even after running for *seven hours* and "looking" at *nearly two billion positions,* the program was still thinking. The stand-alones often couldn't solve the problem quickly either, which surprised us.

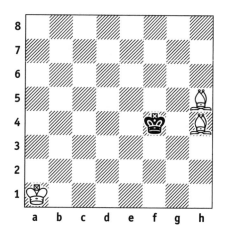

Bishop and Knight vs. King

This is the most difficult of the bare-bones endings. Chances are you'll *never* see it grow out of a real game. We mention it here for the sake of completeness. This mate can be forced, but it is hardly "basic." Even with best play, it can take up to 38 moves! Just in case you're interested: *The correct method against best defense requires three stages. White forces the enemy King to the edge of the board. Then the defender runs to the "wrong" corner—the corner of color opposite to the squares traveled on by the Bishop. Then White forces the defending King—while keeping it on the edge—to the corner square of the same color as the Bishop's terrain.* If you really want to learn this monster, here's a resource: In Chapter 12 you can get information on the Internet Chess Club (www.chessclub.com). They offer frequent on-line lessons on this mate—presumably for insomniacs.

Anyway, the final position looks like this. ▼

**Checkmate!
His Majesty has been driven to the corner that can be controlled by the Bishop. Hemmed in by the Bishop and White King, the Black King is given a leaping check by the Knight. A true team effort!**

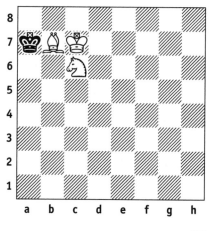

We selected an upscale stand-alone computer rated at an advanced master level, boosted its level considerably, and let it try to mate. It did well in driving our King to the edge, and then to the "wrong color" square, making us edgy as well. But then it showed no understanding of the technique for driving us out of the square. So, no mate, only a draw for the computer.

Certainly, human masters, most experts, and many lower-ranked human players can perform this mate. There's no reason that everyone can't learn it, except that it seems to many an impractical use of time.

> **If you're down in material and see an opportunity to exchange all the pawns to wind up with your lone King against the computer's King, Bishop, and Knight...go for it! If your computer manages to checkmate you, contact us—we'll probably send the programmer a fruit basket!**

So those are the mates that you play when the game has ground down to a few pieces. When one side has an overwhelming superiority, he can mate the opponent's King by brute force. Next comes a mate showing what can happen with more pieces on the board. Sometimes the side that's significantly down in material can pull one out!

Tricked into mate by judo—on the mat in five

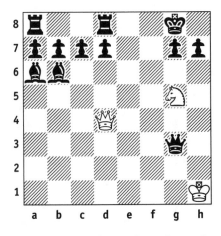

We created this position in order to make our point: The game is not always about material. A quick glance shows that Black has an overwhelming material edge. Not only that, White's Queen is attacked, and if it moves without a check, Black will mate White with 1. ... Qg1.

But White has a knockout that grows right out of the logic of the position: Black's weak a2-g8 diagonal and the powerful locations of White's small army. All you need to know is the special judo throw. It's logical, even though it seems like pure magic!

ChessMaster 5000, set on its mate-solving function, found this *mate-in-five* instantly!

Black's King is exposed. So first White gives check on d5.

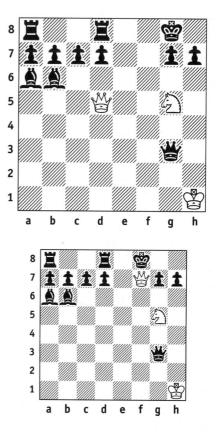

1. Qe5-d5+ ▶

The first feint of the judo master! Now Black must respond to the check and put his own dire threats on hold. If he plays 1. ... Kg8-f8, White mates at once with 2. Qd5-f7, checkmate. That position is good for you to look at, since it shows the Queen and Knight cooperating in a simple checkmate.

In this "what-if" analysis, ▶ Black has walked into a quick checkmate despite his material advantage. But he had another choice back on move 1.

Going back, now, to the larger diagram above, Black makes a better move, one that doesn't walk into immediate mate.

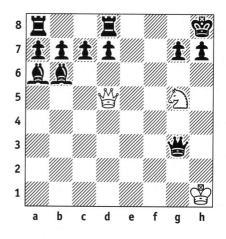

1. Kg8-h8 ▶

Black tucks his King away in the corner. White needs to keep on checking. In fact, the Judo Master can here set up a tactic you will see again in Chapter 4, the usually devastating *discovered check*.

2. Nf7+   Kh8-g8 ▶

Black's last move was forced, but now White has the *discovered check* set up. He can move the Knight almost anywhere, and it will be immune from capture because the Black King will find himself in check from the White Queen!

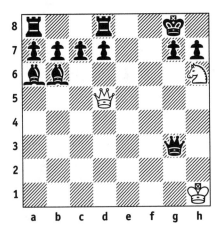

3. Nh6+

Now if White moves to Kf8, he's mated, as in our first what-if analysis, above. So, it's back into the corner!

3. ...   Kg8-h8 ▶

Believe it or not, it's mate in two! One of our favorites, by the way. Remember that the King *can't* move into check. And the goal is to leave him in check and unable to get out.

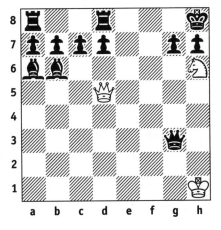

4. Qd5-g8+!!

White would normally find this move because he had run across it before, in a book, or in *postmortems*–after-game discussions–with an experienced player. Our judo master learned the move at his teacher's feet. Maybe you found it on your own!

4. ...   Re8xg8 ▶

Black has no choice but to accept this Queen *sacrifice*. Now White has only his King, which is besieged and confined to a single square, and his Knight, which is under attack by Black's g7-pawn. What do you suggest?

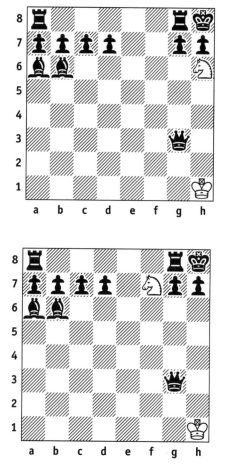

5. Nh6-f7 checkmate!!

It's worth a snapshot of its own. ▶

Mind over matter! Black's King is smothered by White's last piece. And it was all *forced* from the diagram on page 28.

The Black King is *smothered* by his own men and checked by White's last trooper! (Indeed, this kind of mate is called a *smothered mate*.)

Meanwhile, Black's considerable muscle flexes uselessly—in all the wrong places, like a bodybuilder pumping iron in the garage while his wife carries in the groceries.

There are lots of examples we could show of the side with less material winning, and we'll see more examples in Chapter 7, when we look at the *middlegame* of chess. But the *smothered mate* above makes our point for now.

Set up the foregoing positions on your own computer to see how it performs. As we do, first give your computer the stronger side and defend against its mating attempts. Make it as hard as you can for the computer to finish you off. Then set up the position again and take the other side. Checkmate your computer as efficiently as possible. You'll learn a lot about these mating positions that will come in handy later.

And always keep the goal clearly in mind!

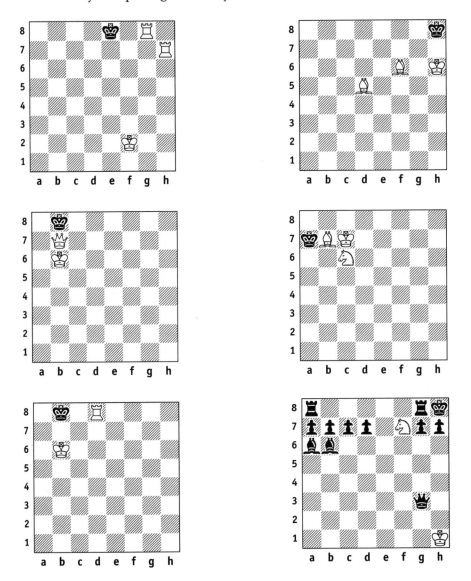

… place your opponent facing the light, which gives you a great advantage. Try to play your adversary when he has just eaten….
–François-André Philidor, best chess player and a leading French operatic composer of the 18th century

Chess is a matter of delicate judgment,
knowing when to punch and how to duck.
—Bobby Fischer

CHAPTER THREE

What's NOT the Goal, but Sometimes Looks Like It!

When you win a chess game, you're awarded one point. When you draw a game, both you and your opponent get a half-point. When you lose, you get a zero. So, whether you're in a formal tournament, or in an informal match of three or four games with a friend, you have an easy way of keeping score.

A couple of situations may look or feel vaguely like wins, but aren't—stalemate and perpetual check. Let's clear up this possible confusion right away. These positions are very useful to know for another reason as well: Knowing them could earn you that half-point, even in a bad position.

Stalemates *aren't* burned-out spouses

Now let's look at a position that is nearly mate, but is scored only as a draw. *Stalemate* occurs when it's one opponent's turn to move, but he can't, and his King is *not* in check. The stalemate is the most disappointing of draws for the stronger side, who has almost, but not quite, overpowered his opponent.

> **If a normal draw is like kissing your sister, a draw by stalemate is like kissing your barber.**

Kamikaze Rook

Sometimes a stalemate surfaces as a wonderfully imaginative swindle. Take a look at this position, which is a version of what chess players

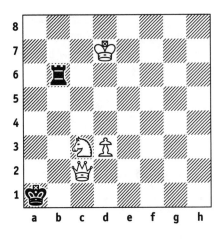

call a "Kamikaze Rook," since the Rook willingly courts death for its emperor.

Notice, at left, that the Black King has no moves. Parodoxically, if he did, his game would be hopeless, given White's menacing superiority. It's Black's move, or White could immediately play 1. Qc2-a2 checkmate. Black can only move his Rook. But if he defends against the mate with 1. ... Rb6-a6, White mates with 2. Qc2-b1. What can Black do?

A mid-range tabletop chess computer—set on a level that makes 60 moves in one hour—couldn't find the right plan. On the other hand, ChessMaster 5000, set on "Expert" level on the same 200 Megahertz Pentium that we used in all the software tests, found the solution almost instantly!

Alan vs. ChessMaster 5000

1.	...	Rb6-d6+!

> **Truly an in-your-face chess move! If White's King takes the undefended and annoying Black Rook, the position is a stalemate—a draw—and White feels justifiably as if he's been caught with his pawns down. All that extra material and no win!**

The Black Rook stays on the sixth rank, checking the White King on the square immediately in front of it. The White King is behind a fence of sorts.

2.	Kd7-e7	Rd6-e6+!
3.	Ke7-f7	Rd6-f6+!
4.	Kf7-g7	Rd6-g6+ ▶

Now you see why the White pawn has to be on d3. It blocks off the Queen from g6. And if White goes to the eight rank, Black's Rook stays on the sixth—it should *never* leave the sixth until White gives up and captures it—checking the White King on the same file.

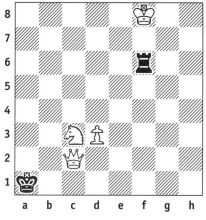

5. Kg7-f8   Rg6-f6+

It's a forever-check, until White takes the Rook, leaving a stalemate, or he moves back and forth on the seventh and eighth ranks until he bumps into three-time repetition or exhausts the 50-move rule—in both cases yielding Black his half-point.

Sometimes a stalemate isn't a flashy save, but the logical outcome of a closely balanced, well played game, like the one on page 55 in the next chapter. ▶

You may get the impression that stalemate isn't fair. After all, the stronger side has *almost* won. Shouldn't he get something better than a draw? In checkers, this situation is a loss for the side that has no legal moves. However, draw by stalemate is one of the possibilities that puts some extra magic into chess. And it's completely logical. Every player starts out knowing the goal. If you don't reach it, you don't win!

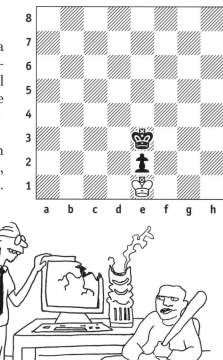

"Draw! Grrrrrrr."

Perps aren't always criminals, and pups don't always have tails

Here's another situation that's very close to a win but isn't. It's called a perpetual check. Chess players call it a "perp" or a "pup." In such a case, one side can check the other side's King at will—forever. If we didn't have rules and if the player were significantly younger than his opponent, he could keep checking and try simply to outlive him. (The technical rule that most often applies here is that when the identical position occurs three times—not necessarily in a row, as some people think—either player can claim a draw, as long as it's done just before executing the move that takes the position to its third incarnation. Another drawing rule, while we're on the subject, is the so-called "50-Move Rule." If 50 moves go by without a pawn move or a piece capture, it's a draw.)

Take a look at these *perps.* Remember, they're all *draws.*

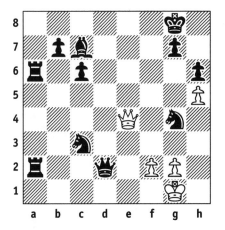

◀ Notice that in this position, Black has an overwhelming material advantage. If White doesn't find a way to keep his opponent busy with checks, Black would immediately begin to bludgeon him into submission. Can you find the perp? Our low-end travel computer didn't. Look what it played!

Basic computer vs. Alan

1. Qe4xg4??
Ouch! This gains a Knight and loses a King!

| 1. | ... | Qd2xf2+ |
| 2. | Kg1-h1 | Ra2-a1 checkmate |

We then tried Fritz, the incredibly powerful software playing program by ChessBase USA. Of course, it took the "pup" in an instant.

From the position in the diagram on page 36:

Fritz vs. Alan

1. **Qe4-e8+**   **Kg8-h7**
2. **Qe6-g6+**   **Kh7-h8**
3. **Qg6-e8+**   **Kh8-h7**

Sure, White just slides his Queen back and forth on the diagonal, splitting the point.

Here's another "pup." In this diagram, Black is way down in material, but he can save the day with checks. Fritz again quickly saw the draw. ▶

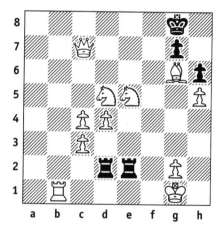

1. **Re2xg2+**

The White King is fenced in on the first rank, and wherever it goes, this Rook will check him, protected by his twin, who must stay anchored. Take White against your computer to confirm this.

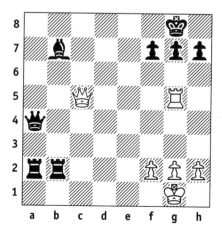

Sometimes a player who is otherwise losing finds a way to sacrifice a piece to make a pup possible. Can you see a possibility for that here?

◀ We set this position up on Battle Chess. It found the following save:

1. **Rg5xg7+!**

Black must take the Rook. His only "option," 1. ... Kg8-h8, gives White an immediate mate with 2. Qf8.

1.	...	Kg8xg7
2.	Qg5+	▶

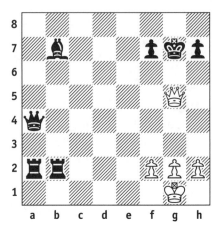

Now, whether the harassed King moves to h8 or f8, White simply slides his Queen to d8 and checks Black perpetually on the diagonal d8 to g5.

In these examples, when the side that's down heaps of material saves the day with a "surprise," you can see that the main forces of the materially superior side stand awkwardly watching the action from afar. Keeping pieces "in reserve" is a sure way to lose at chess! Get your forces working together and into the game!

Stalemates and perpetual checks are *not* the ultimate goal. But knowing them comes in handy, both to avoid them when you're winning and to try for them when you're way behind!

The move is there, but you must see it.
– Savielly Tartakover

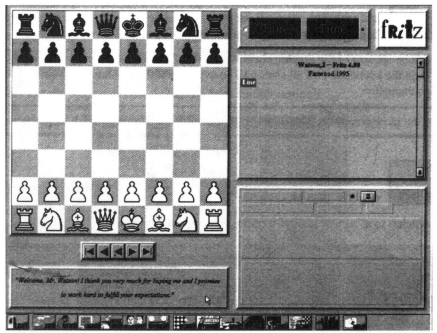

If you want to win at chess,
begin with the ending.
—Irving Chernev

CHAPTER FOUR

Beginning Near the End

You have to be one of us, a Homo Sapiens—a wise man or woman—to really "get" chess. To be sure, it's a game of calculation, at which computers excel. But it's also clearly a game where understanding and applying basic principles—in combination with our abilities to be both methodical and inspired—give humans an advantage.

But, as they say, that's the talk. Now let's walk the walk. Actually, let's take a King walk that will support what you've just read—and teach you a great deal about chess in just a few pages.

Three games in one

You can save yourself a lot of frustration if you learn to see chess as a game in three phases. The pieces move exactly the same in each phase, and each phase shares some guiding principles in common. But each phase also has its own helpful principles.

Phase 1: The Opening
Phase 2: The Middlegame
Phase 3: The Endgame

Endgames have their own logic—Kings like to fight!

As the greatest chess champions and the greatest chess teachers overwhelmingly recommend, we're going to begin with the last phase of the game. Boxing has its "championship rounds," the 11th and 12th, where a tough, close match among peers is often decided. Football has its two-minute offense, an all-out attack that can change the outcome of the grueling near-hour of play that came before.

Likewise, in chess, the endgame is a time when you can reap the rewards of your opening and middlegame play, or blow it all, letting your opponent get away with a draw, or even turn the tables completely, winning a "lost" game! Despite the well-known advantages of studying the endgame, most players–even tournament competitors–ignore all the good advice, and are therefore at their weakest in this important phase. (It's as if they want to be successful musicians but refuse to practice the scales!) So you see them, again and again, failing to reap the reward of their good moves that went before. That's why, with a sound knowledge of guiding endgame principles, you will have a tremendous advantage–against man *or* machine! For it turns out that programmers also often ignore the endgame!

So beginning at the end provides the right focus: The endgame, or "ending," is the judgment day of chess. And starting with a careful look at the endgame also gets you used to how to use the pieces and the pawns. (Chess players accept a class structure on the board; the armies are divided into pawns, the eight little foot soldiers on each side that the French literally call "peons," and that the Germans call "farmers," and the eight other, more valuable men. But chess players are still, often, human and we at times refer to the whole army as "pieces." when we should say "men.") Playing endings of different kinds gives you a feel for how different elements of your army work together the most effectively, and what the scope of each piece is.

> **The endgame is the Judgment Day of chess. The King gives a command and a promise at the beginning of the game to his most humble subjects, the pawns. "Go forth first into the danger of battle. But you who reach the other side will have a share in my kingdom. You shall become Queen."**

King and pawn endings

Let's take a look at a "simple" position that any chess player worth his score pad–the little notepad we record our important games on–*should* know by heart, but many don't. And I'll bet your computer doesn't have much of a clue either!

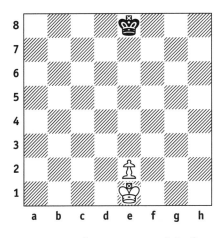

White has an extra pawn. If it reaches the opposite side of the board, it will become a Queen. Then forcing checkmate will be a matter of very simple technique. Can White force a win if it's his move? What happens if Black moves first? What are the basic strategies?

It can't get simpler than this, can it? If there was no pawn remaining, the game would of course be a draw. The Kings can't even check each other–they would be moving into check themselves, and that's illegal–let alone give checkmate. Like two real Kings without armies, they would have to co-exist forever, without further fighting. But the lowly "peon" makes all the difference. Granted, he can't do much in his present state, but remember the King's promise to his pawns!

The plot of most endgames revolves around queening a pawn.

The question is whether the White King can shepherd one of his lowly subjects to the other end of the board and its coronation as a full-fledged Queen. Along the way the Black King will, of course, try to capture it. Failing that, he will try to block its "queening" square. Use your set-up mode to duplicate the position in the above diagram.

First let's take a look at how a middle-of-the-road, hand-held computer "defends" the position. We'll take the White side and simply follow one of the important guiding principles that we know applies to this kind of *endgame.*

In King and pawn endings, where the defending King can reach the queening square before the pawn can, the superior side should advance his own King *ahead of* the pawn, toward the ultimate queening square, as far as possible without being cut off from the pawn's defense.

By the way, in the opening or middlegame, with squadrons of heavy artillery still roaming the board, this same principle would lead to instant disaster. Such a King errant would wind up checkmated in the middle of the board. So advancing your King is a special principle for the *endgame*.

Okay, looking at this position, we can see that the Black King is already *on* our pawn's queening square. Our little soldier can only move straight ahead unless he's capturing–so the above rule certainly applies. So here we go, just following our simple rule.

Human vs. basic hand-held computer

1. Ke1-f2   Ke8-d7
The White King leaves his pawn in reserve, first advancing to secure territory. The Black King moves to meet its counterpart.

2. Kf2-e3   Kd7-d6
Black would put up stiffer resistance–the key to saving many lost positions–by laying back on the seventh rank. Then, when White's King came to the fourth rank, Black could *take the opposition.*

Let's stop, in fact, to *analyze* that possibility, after White's last move. ▶

2. ...   Kd7-e7
3. Ke3-e4   Ke7-e6

The Kings stand in *opposition* at right. The King who must give way gives ground. Unfortunately for Black, White has played correctly, advancing his King ahead of his pawn. ▶

◀ Now White simply plays.

4. e2-e3!
And White takes back the opposition. Black must give way, and White will be able to force his pawn to the queening square. We'll see how this works in a bit.

Our analysis of what the computer *didn't* play taught us even more about the opposition, and showed us that Black could have defended with greater resolve.

Now back to the *real* game, human vs. computer.

3. Ke3-d4 ▶
White "takes the opposition," one of the most important ideas in the tool box of the endgame craftsman. Black must move his King–either to the side or backward–and lose the face-off.

3. ... Kd6-e6
Here we're going to slide over and take the opposition again. Whenever possible, we want to operate directly in front of our pawn.

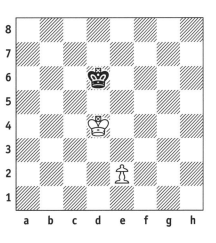

4. Kd4-e4 Ke6-d6
So the computer slides to the side again. This time, we play for the end run, while remembering that we don't want to let the Black King get to our pawn before we can defend it.

5. Ke4-f5   Kd6-d5

Again, not the stiffest resistance. Black would be better off staying close to the only square that can defeat him: e8. (See where simple human logic, applied thoughtfully, helps cut through the maze?) Now we're at a crossroads. We could make a terrible move—6. Kf6??—a mistake that would throw away the whole game. Black could then play 6. ... Ke4!, and we could not save our only hope for a win, the pawn we left behind! The Black King would simply move forward and capture it while we watched helplessly. So...

6. e2-e4+   ▶

The pawn uses its first-move option to advance two squares, giving check and forcing the Black King to give ground again. Meanwhile, the White King has taken up a strategic location that prevents his royal opposite from moving back in the pawn's direct path!

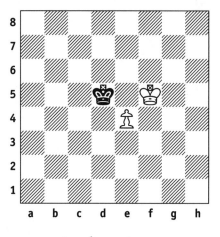

Now the Black King doesn't have e6, getting directly in front of the pawn, because White's King controls that square. So Black must move somewhere else. What does your computer choose?

6. ...   Kd5-d4?

It's true that Black is already lost to best play by White—play that can be found by adhering to our simple principles. But this move shows a lack of understanding. Black gives up completely. His only remote hope is to fall back as close to the queening square as possible, and hope White errs.

Our computer opponent's choice also reveals the *horizon effect*. Because a computer doesn't have our comforting human principles to rely on, it must base its course completely on calculating moves. It can only "visualize" a small number of lines—depending on the level it is set on—so it runs away from the center of the action. In that way its sure and ultimate defeat is over its horizon. Like an ostrich with its head in the sand, it sees no danger and feels safe.

The rest really is easy.

7. e4-e5   Kd4-d5
8. Kf5-f6   Kd5-d4

9. e5-e6   Kd4-e4 ▶

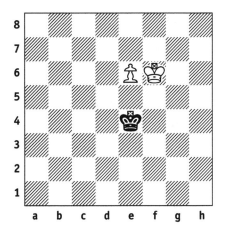

Now the coast is clear to e8 and White's pawn can high-step to his promotion, even without its King to help.

We can chalk up a win here. The computer will keep playing. The horizon effect prevents it from "seeing" its ultimate checkmate, so it will continue to play when a human, with judgment, can see that the contest is over.

The human knows the game is a foregone conclusion. He applies logic. He knows the pawn will queen and he knows that he can then force checkmate. The computer, who is number-crunching, doesn't "see" his specific demise, so appears to wander around in a happy-go-lucky daze, waiting for the safe to fall on him. We won't indulge him, because we have other points to make. In our superior human fashion, we'll press the "NEW GAME" key. But when this kind of position occurs in your games against your computer, play the game out to practice your mating routines.

The final position in the above game is an opportunity to point out another cornerstone of endgame play: the "Rule of the Square." Let's take the White King out of the picture completely, and insert drawn lines to indicate the square. The Rule of the Square tells you at a glance if a King can catch an unsupported enemy pawn before it reaches its queening square.

If the King, *on move*, can get into the square, it can stop the pawn. Here, it's clear that the King can't catch the pawn.

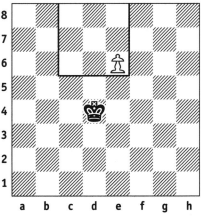

> **The Rule of the Square calculation aid can make others think you have a computer for a brain. Actually, you do—and it's a better one than any chess computer.**

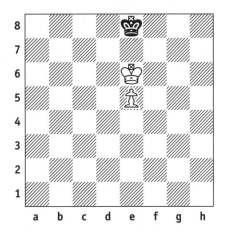

If it's Black's move, can he catch the pawn? If it's White's move, can he queen?

Answer: Yes, and yes. The Rule of the Square is a great shortcut. You can develop this into a regular parlor trick if you want to. Didn't you think chess masters had tricks of the trade?

The "I Win" position

Here's another handy shortcut. ▶

In King and Pawn endgames, any time a side reaches this position (King on sixth rank, immediately ahead of his pawn) he wins, no matter whose move it is and where the enemy King is. The only exception is when the extra pawn is a Rook pawn.

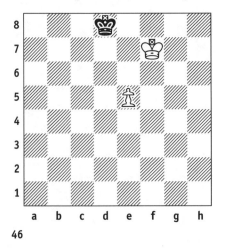

◀ If it's Black's move, he must play to the side, letting our King in. For example, if he plays 1. ... Ke8-d8, we'd move 2. Ke6-f7.

White controls the queening square. The pawn waltzes in for its coronation. As we know, the Queen and King will checkmate a lone King easily.

If White is to move in the "I Win" position (middle diagram, previous page), here's how it goes: 1. Ke6-d6 Ke8-d8 2. e5-e6 Kd8-e8...

This is the position that the superior side wants as he approaches the next-to-last rank and is on move. The pawn will advance. ▶

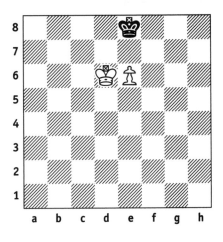

3. e6-e7 Ke8-f7 4. Kd6-d7– and again the pawn will become Queen-for-a-Game.

The important thing about knowing the "I Win" position on the page opposite is that it gives you a paradigm for winning many positions. If you can reach this position, regardless of whose move it will be, you know you'll win–case closed. Your dismayed opponent and the impressed onlookers may think you had to calculate all the way to queening. No need to enlighten them! Let 'em read this book.

If you work awhile with the position in the diagram on page 41, at the beginning of this chapter, you'll conclude that, on move, White can force the "I Win" position, unless Black accepts an even worse position with his King offside. In other words, that diagram, showing the Kings staring balefully at each across an empty board except for a White pawn on e2 with White to move, is what chessers call a "forced win" for White. If it's Black's move, he can draw.

The other side of the King and Pawn game

So, we've proved, so far, that the computer played a poor defense in an already lost position. Now let's go back to our original idea and give Black (the computer) the extra pawn and the move. The position is a mirror image of the diagram on page 41. As chess players would say, colors are reversed. Once again, use your set-up option. Make sure that, before leaving set-up mode, you follow the manufacturer's directions to leave Black on move. Here's what our same model did.

The computer begins with a won position. We know the guiding principle: He should advance his King as far as possible before advancing his pawn. Let the chip show what he's got! ▶

Human vs. basic computer

1. ...   Ke8-d7

Uh-oh. This good move gave us pause. The machine is a brand-new model, rushed to us from the manufacturer for this book. Previous models from the same manufacturer erred immediately. Will we have to rewrite this chapter, avoiding our superior attitude? Well, let's play the best defense and make him beat us, if he can. That's the stuff that saves games.

2. Ke1-e2   e7-e5??

No, our text can stand. This horrible move, showing no understanding of the logic of the position, throws away the win. Now note the repeated sequence Black must use to force White backward so that the pawn can advance without capture. And understand that it forces Black, without any reasonable option, to reach the next-to-last rank in the precise configuration he winds up with here.

3. Ke2-e3   Kd7-d6
4. Ke3-e4   Kd6-e6

Here's the first occurrence of the upcoming pattern. ▼

The **"Going Nowhere"** position. The extra pawn at right is going nowhere–regardless of who is to move. Black has an extra pawn, but will move it down the board only to find a big disappointment.

5. Kd4-e3   Ke6-d5
6. Ke3-d3   e5-e4+
7. Kd3-e3   Kd5-e5

Here's that "Going Nowhere" position again, moved down the board one rank. Notice how White follows an important pattern. He drops back, opposes the Black King, forcing Black to check him with the pawn in order to advance.

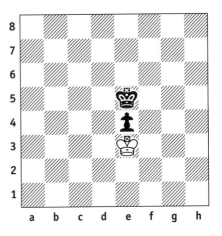

8. Ke3-e2

Other moves, such as Kf2 or Kd2, would also draw, but it's best to get into the habit of dropping back, when you have to, on the same file as the enemy pawn.

8. ... Ke5-d4

Here's a key moment. It's still easy for White to make a mistake and lose. He's on a tightrope. But if he knows where to put his feet, he'll never hit the ground.

9. Ke2-d2 ▶

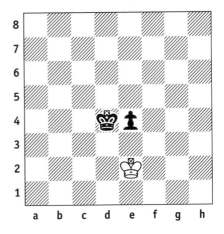

This is the *only* move. For example, 9. Ke2-f2, or King to any square dropping backward, loses, because Black can eventually take control of the queening square. (Notice that 9. Ke2-f2 Kd4-d3 10. K-anywhere, and Black has 10. ... Kd3-e3, achieving the "I Win" position!) Once that happens, it's over. We made the right move because we know how to keep the "Going Nowhere" position going nowhere. But we could have found it by applying this simple principle. (When it was its turn with White, the computer demonstrated it couldn't apply this rule!)

In endgames, when you're forced to move your King, always keep in front of the enemy pawn or King. Never move to the side, and never, *ever*, move *backward*–unless you absolutely have to. Use your King to block.

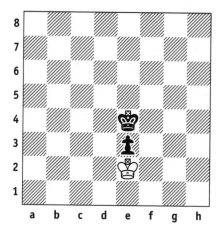

| 9. ... | e4-e3+ |
| 10. Kd2-e2 | Kd4-e4 |

◀

11. Ke2-e1
When you're *forced* to move backward in such an endgame, play back along the pawn's file.

| 11. ... | Ke4-d3 |
| 12. Ke1-d1 ▼ | |

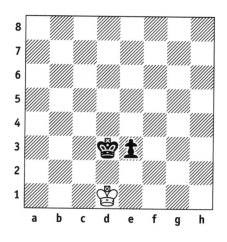

Here we are again. You're about to see another solid-gold endgame principle in action. In such positions, if the pawn hits the next-to-last rank *with check*, it's a draw because of the stalemate motif! If you're the one with the extra pawn, try to advance your pawn to this rank *without* giving check!

| 12. ... | e3-e2+ |

There's the check.

13. Kd1-e1   Kd3-4(!?)
Whoa! The computer makes a highly logical move...from its point of view as a silicon space cadet. Let's delve into its "logic." A human player would play 1. ... Kd3-e3 here, creating the stalemate we predicted.

"Logic, logic, logic, lo...!"

Here's where the "Going Nowhere" position has led —nowhere! Stalemate occurs when one King must move, but can't—but isn't in check. (That last detail makes all the difference! It's a draw, a half-point in chess.)

So our computer makes the "best move," in a way, by wandering away from the pawn, moving his King to d4. After all, his human opponent may get a telephone call from the IRS, become distracted thinking about all the receipts he didn't save, and move his King to f2 and then g3, out of the pawn's square, and lose. Of course, this is silly. White captures the pawn the second Black abandons it, and the game is an immediate draw by the rules of chess, because there is insufficient mating material.

More pawns

Let's take a look, at right, at what can happen when more than one pawn is on the board.

With Black to move, he can immediately secure the draw (which he should do, since he is material down—anything else complicates his drawing chances). He should play:

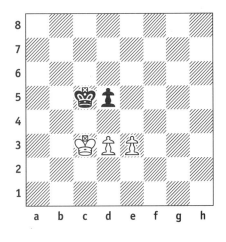

| 1. | ... | d5-d4+! |
| 2. | e3xd4 | |

White would like to play e3-e4, moving his pawn toward the queening square, but it's check, and he must capture.

| 2. | ... | Kc5-d5 |

The Black King "sacrificed" his last pawn, and even put himself in check to get this position. After White moves to Kc3-d2, Black achieves the "Going Nowhere" position! Even "simple" pawn positions can contain little traps and chess "jokes" like this one.

Let's add another pawn to each side. ▶

Here Black is lost! The material deficit remains exactly the same—one little farmer, as our German colleagues would say. But the *total number* of the pawns makes the difference. Let's look at the defense that made it so easy in the previous example.

1.	...	d5-d4+
2.	e3xd4+	e5xd4+
3.	Kc3-b3	

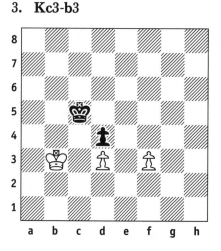

White's pawn on the f-file is an outside *passed pawn*. There are no pawns occupying or controlling any of the squares between it and its queening square. A passed pawn is a dangerous peon!

This time it's the White King's turn to step coolly to the side and wait! White will win easily by pushing his *passed* f-pawn. When Black's King runs to catch it, White's King will capture the Black pawn on d4 and wind up with his King on the sixth.

White has reached the "I Win" position! ▶

52

> With one side ahead by one pawn, the more pawns on the board, the more likely it is that the extra pawn wins by force. The winning side forces a *passed pawn* and pushes it. It will queen, or it will *decoy* the defending King, leaving his other pawns undefended.

Breakthrough

There's a well-known and intriguing pawn formation that humans discovered over the centuries. We call it the "breakthrough."

It's White's move, in the position at right. Unless White has a trick, Black's King will cakewalk back to White's pawns and pick them off, getting an easily won game, because he could then promote his own. There *is* a trick, and a mid-range, tabletop computer, set on one minute per move, found it very quickly!

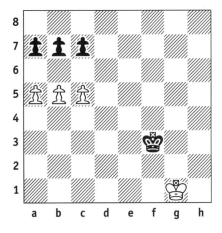

1. b6!

This move wins in all variations because a White pawn breaks through to its queening square.

1. ...   a7xb6
2. c5-c6!   ▶

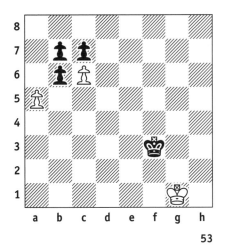

The idea: If Black captures the c-pawn, White advances the now unchallenged, unstoppable a-pawn. If Black takes the a-pawn, White captures the Black pawn on b7 with his c-pawn, and this little farmer is looking at a big promotion!

Going back to the diagram at the top of the previous page, let's suppose it's Black's move. If he doesn't do something about the pawn formation, White will play b5-b6 and win as we have just seen. So what does Black do? The same computer, now playing Black, again found the right move, at once.

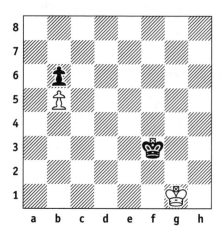

1. ...   **b7-b6!**
Again, the key move. Black blocks White from the square.

2. a5xb6   **a7xb6**
3. c5xb6   **c7xb6** ▶
Black's King will scoot back to win the White pawn, but the game will be a draw with best play. The best Black can do is to achieve the position in the diagram below.

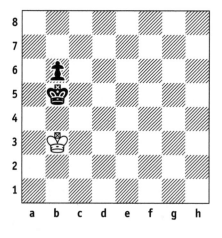

White has just played his King to b3. This will lead directly to the "Going Nowhere" position!

Try it yourself. Make a number of attempts, playing the best you can for both sides. And defend the White side against your computer. You'll see that Black can't achieve the "I Win" position, with his King on the third rank, and his pawn behind it–unless you make a defensive mistake. You can learn a lot by playing these kinds of position against your computer.

Quality vs. Quantity

We all like to have extra pawns in an ending. But you can see that their *quality* is often more important than their *quantity*. Take a look at this next position. White can draw easily. Do you see how?

White simply moves 1. Kg3-f2, then to f1. Then he moves back and forth between these two squares. Black's King is trapped, immobile, in the corner. All he can do is shuffle his quadrupled and isolated pawns ahead until he runs out of pawn moves and is stalemated! Give your computer Black and play it out—just to feel superior. You can even honestly tell your friends you gave your chess computer a seven-pawn handicap in the endgame and drew it easily! Hmm. Perhaps that's the makings of a good bet with someone who thinks computers are invincible!

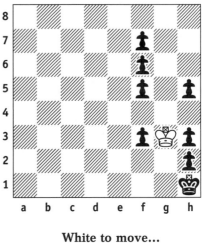

White to move...
and not to panic!

The relative value of the chess men

You can't make informed decisions about chess moves unless you know their relative values. It turns out that keeping these values in mind is very easy. Although there are 32 chessmen on the board at the beginning of the game, there are only SIX different kinds of pieces, including the King! This little chart below says just about everything on the topic. If you assign a value of one to the most insignificant peon of a chess man, the pawn, you get this:

Relative Value of the Chess Men		
Pawn	♟	1
Knight	♞	3
Bishop	♝	3
Rook	♜	5
Queen	♛	9
King	♚	Infinitely valuable

Exchanging men

Many exchanges are unavoidable. But when you intentionally trade a piece, make sure you do so with a purpose in mind, such as when you can see that you can get to a superior endgame. And don't trade one of your men for one of your enemy's men of less value, unless you have a *very* good reason! Computer opponents are particularly good at getting this kind of *material advantage* and holding on to it until the endgame. Here's a very useful general rule about exchanges that will help you win when you're ahead, or draw when you're behind! (Remember that pawns aren't pieces.)

> **If you're ahead in material, trade *pieces*.**
> **If you're behind in material, trade *pawns!***

After all, it's very frequently those little peons that are the payoff. The chess player ahead in material wants to hang on to his pawns to queen them in the endgame just as a Las Vegas gambler on a winning streak wants to horde his chips for the big cash-in. Take a look at the position in the diagram to the right, which presses our last principle immediately into action.

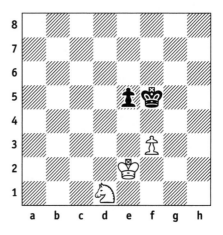

Black is down a whole Knight— the equivalent of about three pawns. So Black should trade *pawns*. ▶

1. ...   e5-e4

White is forced to trade pawns or lose his pawn for nothing. The game is a dead draw. As we know, lonely Knight can't mate!

If White is to move, he wins by *preventing* the exchange of pawns with Ke2-e3. Now if Black tries e5-e4, White captures when his own pawn protected. The Knight *is* capable of working with the King to shepherd the pawn to its queening square!

Rook and pawn endings

These are the most common endgames. So it's very practical to understand some guiding principles specifically about these endings.

> **Rook and pawn endings are among the most drawish. If you're down in pawns, keep the Rooks on the board!**

Philidor's position

André Philidor correctly analyzed this next position in the 18th century. He worked out a method that draws easily, illustrating the drawing power of the Rook. His work is now a basic part of every master's knowledge.

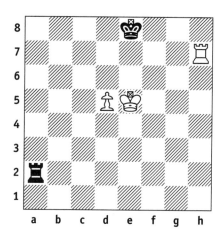

Black draws easily if he knows the method. Black prevents White's King from advancing in *front* of his pawn to the sixth rank. White is forced to advance his pawn to get shelter from the Rook. At that point, Black shifts his Rook to the first rank, behind the King and pawn, and gives checks from there. With the White pawn on the sixth rank, White's King can't hide from these checks, and so White won't be able to drive the Black King from its defense of the queening square. Play could go like this:

1. ...   Ra2-a6!
Black prevents White's King going to the sixth rank, and waits for the pawn to advance.

2. d5-d6   Ra1
3. Kd5-e6   Ra1-e1+
White can't make progress because of the distant checks. He can't hide in front of his own pawn, because it is now too close to the Black King, which blocks his way.

Both our mid-range tabletop and hand-held models failed to defend this position properly as Black. They both made the same mistake, playing 1. ... Ra2-f2?; and after 2. Ke5-e6, White threatens mate and has the d6 square to hide from checks from behind. The Black King must move away from the queening square, and White chaperones his pawn to its promotion. Alan got to win a few games! Then ChessMaster 5000 showed us how Black should defend. Practice defending as Black and try to win as White against your computer. You'll get this ending down pat after a little practice.

This next example illustrates a very important principle of Rook and Pawn endings.

> **Rooks belong behind the passed pawn, whether the pawn is yours or your opponent's.**

If it is White's move, he plays 1. Rd5-d1!, with the simple but strong idea of playing the Rook to b1, where it supports the advance of his b-pawn. In front of the pawn, Black's Rook makes a poor defender. White has a big edge.

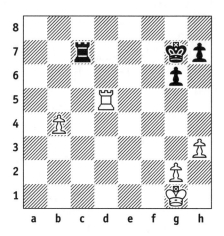

If it is Black's move, he plays 1. ... Rc2 or ... Rc1+ with the same idea, getting to b1. From here his Rook makes it hard for the pawn to advance safely. The position is a likely draw.

Our mid-range expert-rated computer didn't find the technique at the 60-moves-in-60-minute level. As White it played 1. b4-b5, and Alan was able to draw easily with 1. ... Rc7-c1+, getting behind the pawn. Even ChessMaster 5000 at Expert level failed the test, playing the same move.

Our chess computers didn't do well with Rook and pawn endings, the most common type of endgame. One way to play to beat your computer is to head for this kind of ending whenever possible. Practice them often against your computer. It won't learn, but you will!

"In this corner...2000 lbs. of memory-chips, controller chips and the latest high-tech software! And in the..."

Bishop and pawn endings— Opposite-color Bishops

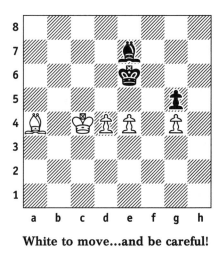

White to move...and be careful!

The most drawish endings in chess theory fall under this ending—*if the opponent's Bishops travel on different colors.* Look at the position at right.

Even ahead by two connected, passed pawns, White must play carefully. A mistake that irretrievably throws away the win is 1. d5+??, because after 1. ... Ke6-d6 2. Be8, Black will play 2. ... Be7-f6, with an unshakable blockade.

This technique is called "building a fortress." Black's pieces can't be driven away once they own the dark squares in front of the pawns, because White's Bishop can't "reach" them—no matter how close it gets!

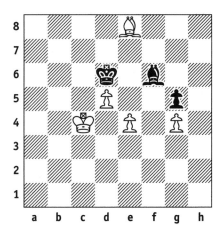

Black has blockaded White's extra pawns on the dark squares. Because White's Bishop can't challenge these squares, Black can't be forced out of his *fortress.*

Our chatty mid-range stand-alone found the *correct* plan as White: 1. e4-e5!, advancing on the dark squares, preventing the fortress position. White will use his Bishop and King to drive the Black King out of the way, and the pawns will advance, always leading with an advance on the dark squares! White wins.

Opposite-color Bishops are extremely drawish. You can sometimes "build a fortress" to safely hold back a number of your opponent's extra pawns.

Like-color Bishops

These endings, on the other hand, hold no special propensity to be drawish. However, with only one pawn on the board, as in the example to the right, there are always chances for a draw.

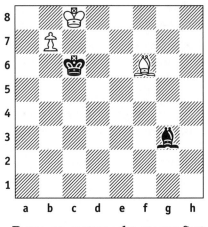

Draw, no matter who moves first

Black's Bishop can't be driven off the h2-b8 diagonal. Black moves his Bishop back and forth on this diagonal, leaving his King on c6, so that White can't play Bd8-c7. If White pushes his pawn to b8, Black will simply capture it. Since a King and Bishop can't checkmate, it's a draw.

This second example shows that, with more pawns on the board, even though Black's deficit is still just one pawn, White often wins. White has an extra, outside passed pawn—a passed pawn away from the rest of the pawns on the board. These are extremely powerful tools, since they divert defenders.

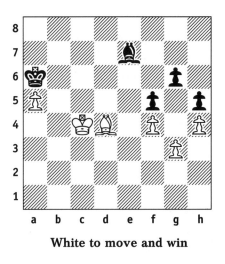

White to move and win

White has a simple but unstoppable plan. He plays his Bishop to c3 and then e1. On e1 his Bishop guards his pawn on a5 and his pawn on g3. Then his King heads for f7. Black's Bishop can't defend the Black kingside pawns, nor can it keep out the enemy King, who will travel on the a2-g8, light-square diagonal. If the Black King tries to come to the aid of his kingside, White advances his a-pawn.

Playing White on the 60/60 level, our mid-range stand-alones did not find the winning procedure. ChessMaster found it very quickly, as did the powerful Fritz software.

Knights in the endgame

The Knight is a short-range piece. On the edge of the board, this weakness is highlighted. Compare the Knight and Bishop in the position at right.

The Bishop radiates power, while the Knight is trapped on the edge: "on the rim is dim" per Dr. Tarrasch.

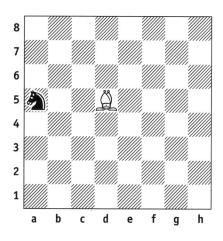

In the next position, we can see the vulnerability of the Knight on the edge of the board in a practical position.

White has a quick and forced win here, based on the Knight's restricted mobility when it is on the edge. Can you find the move?

White plays 1. Rb1xb7+! After 1. ... Nd6xb7 2. a5-a6, Black can't stop the pawn! A middle-of-road tabletop found this line in under one minute. So did all the software programs. Play it out. You'll never forget about the Knight's weakness on the edge of the board!

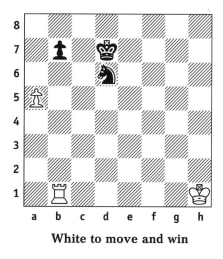

White to move and win

Queen endings with pawns

When the Queens are on the board, almost anything can happen.

> **One generalization we can make is that, in endings with Queens and pawns, the *quality* of the pawns is more important than the *quantity* of pawns.**

Even two pawns down, White wins simply by advancing his advanced, outside passed pawn. Even if it were Black's move, he would be in trouble!

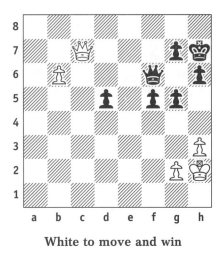

White to move and win

Software programs, tabletops, and hand-held models all found 1. b6-b7. It's not a difficult move to find, but it makes the case for *quality* over *quantity* in Queen endings with pawns!

The passed pawn is a criminal, who should be kept under lock and key.
Mild measures, such as police surveillance, are not sufficient.
—Aaron Nimzovitch

In chess there is only one mistake: over-estimation of your opponent. All else is either bad luck or weakness.

–Savielly Tartakover

CHAPTER FIVE

An Insider's View of the Great Chips-Byte-Man Story

Don Maddox, a former editor of *Chess Life Magazine*, is now president of ChessBase USA. His company specializes in chess-training software and provided training support to both Deeper Blue and to Garry Kasparov. Most of the world's best players use ChessBase (a games storage and retrieval system) and Fritz5 (a world-class playing program), and so do thousands of amateurs worldwide.

Don's computer databases allow you–on just your home computer–to find, for example, all the master games on file that reached a position you're researching. And to find what happened afterward! Or, even more quickly, these discs containing hundreds of thousands of games can be made to provide you with the precise game you're looking for. If chess hadn't made us so logical, we'd have to think Maddox simply distributes magic. To paraphrase a journalist writing of the great Akiba Rubinstein after the Polish master had forced a win in an endgame position formerly thought to be unwinnable: In an earlier century, Don would have been burned at the stake as a sorcerer.

Don worked with the Deep Blue team to build the critical database of games for both its 1996 and 1997 matches against Professional Chess Association World Champ Garry Kasparov. Don's the one who compiled the "book"–Deep Blue's awesome memory of previously played master chess games and their results. Many speculate that Kasparov–widely held to be the strongest player of all time–cracked during the match under the specter of the "memory" Don provided to the supercomputer components in Deep Blue.

In this exclusive interview by co-author Al Lawrence with the man who compiled Deeper Blue's memory, Maddox gives us the ultimate insider's view of man-against-chess-machine. Al's questions and comments are set off and in *italics*.

Don, in early May, 1997, a small team of computer scientists working for IBM—backed up by you and American International Grandmaster Joel Benjamin—accomplished the impossible: They defeated World Chess Champion Garry Kasparov at his own game, across the chessboard. The obvious question: Why did Kasparov lose this match against Deeper Blue, making him the first World Champion to lose a match to a computer?

Before we can answer the questions of why Kasparov lost and what it means to us and the rest of humanity, we have to talk a little bit about computers and chess in general. Not so many years ago, experts were saying that computers would never play at master level (the top two percent of tournament players), much less at grandmaster level (probably the top half percent of all masters).

Why is chess so hard for computers to play?

Let's look at the arithmetic. An early computer chess pioneer, Claude E. Shannon, calculated the possible moves in a chess game to exceed the number of atoms in the known universe. His figure translates into 10 to the 120th power. Shannon pointed out that if a computer could calculate one 40-move game per microsecond (and Deep Blue can't) it would take the program 10 to the 90th power years to make its first move. Not your ideal spectator sport!

Good grief! That must be longer than my typical lunch break! But we've all read that these computers "think" so fast!

Deeper Blue, light-years ahead of earlier chess-playing computers, calculates 200 million positions a second—50 billion positions in three minutes! As spectacular as that sounds, these numbers are dwarfed in Shannon's awe-inspiring chess universe.

The point is that chess is *too big* for today's—or tomorrow's—computers to *solve*. The good news for computers is that Deep Blue doesn't have to solve chess to play the game. That's where heuristics come in. A computer doesn't have to look at every move—it can eliminate "obvious" losers and concentrate on "reasonable" candidate moves. The problem is that chess is a game of exceptions, and every pruned branch is a line that might lead to triumph or disaster down the road.

As a human, I have to tell you I love the horizon effect in computers. In a comic vein, it seems almost as if we've created the robotic version of Gone With the Wind's Scarlett O'Hara, whose favorite phrase when faced with unavoidable danger is "I can't think about that today. I'll think about that tomarraw!" Only, I suppose Deeper Blue has an Ivy League accent.

Yes, to make matters worse, computers can evaluate only positions they actually *see*, that are within their *horizon*. If checkmate occurs one move beyond that horizon, it is invisible to them until the next move pushes the horizon out another half-move or two—generally too late to save the hapless machine from a blunder. Deeper Blue is designed to push its horizon further out in lines that threaten the King, but the supercomputer is as vulnerable to the *horizon effect* as any other computer in more subtle, less dramatic positions.

So what makes chess hard for computers is its vastness and their virtual obligation to examine every line and every position before making a decision. With unlimited time and a perfect evaluation algorithm, these disadvantages disappear. But against Garry, Deep Blue had only three minutes a move, and its evaluation algorithm is "constantly improving"—corporate key words for "far from perfect."

If chess is so hard for computers, why are they so hard to beat?
One way to answer is that computers don't have to play very well to beat most human beings!

They'd better look out after enough people read this book!
I think you're right! But even PC-based programs now routinely "see" several moves ahead on a fast machine. Within their horizon, they see virtually everything, they don't blunder away material, and they take advantage of your every mistake. In fact, they are forced to *win* very few games; human beings *lose* a lot of them.

And they have a perfect memory for whatever opening moves people like you put into their brains!
Yes, today's programs are delivered with a strong *openings book* installed. This "book" contains a database of theoretical openings material, often "tuned" to guide play into positions the program plays well! As long as play follows these book lines, the program doesn't have to "think" at all—it spits back known responses instantaneously and without reflection. During the book phase of the game, the program is literally immune to any form of memory error, while its human opponent struggles along the best he or she can, risking a catastrophic mistake with every decision. Many players—as Garry did in Game 6—end up with a lost position before their electronic opponent ever moves out of its book.

The corollary is that computers don't have to play chess as well as human beings to produce similar results. Why? Because they are essentially opportunistic beasts programmed to deny their opponents the same opportunities—like tennis automatons incapable of unforced errors, they feed on your mistakes without returning the favor.

One thing we can certainly learn from chess computers is their "attitude" in bad positions. I don't know how many times I've gotten over-confident in a winning position against them!

Chess-playing computers defend tenaciously. In a bad position, most human beings eventually crumble psychologically and self-destruct. A computer simply churns out the best moves it can find, oblivious to the ruin of its position until it's mated or its opponent makes a mistake. You are unlikely to see Deep Blue resign a drawn position, as Garry did in Game 2.

Finally, we humans are our own worst enemies at the chessboard. Human beings get nervous and tired; they overlook obvious moves, lose their objectivity, and give up hope—all sins the computer is immune to.

Is that what happened to Garry in this match?

Any strong players going over the games from this match know that Garry played "better" chess than Deep Blue; anyone looking at the final score knows it didn't matter!

Look, does any of this state-of-the-art research have much to do with you and me playing our home computers a game of chess?

Remarkably enough, Garry Kasparov lost to Deep Blue the same way you can lose to your own computer at home, and there are clear lessons to be learned from his defeat.

First, in advance of the match, he *underestimated* Deeper Blue as a whole. At the same time, he *overestimated* its opening book. The result was a misplaced confidence in an opening strategy that stressed getting the computer "out of book" early. My work on Deep Blue's database of games and much of Grandmaster Joel Benjamin's work on its opening book went virtually unchallenged until Garry stumbled catastrophically out of book in Game 6.

As a result, Garry played a series of decidedly un-Kasparov-like openings throughout the match, religiously avoiding book lines with White and his own active repertoire with Black. Kasparov's advisors may argue the strategy was a success. He won Game 1, should have drawn Game 2, and ended up with dangerous advantages in Games 3, 4 and 5. Game 6 hardly counts—except to the score. But he also built up large deficits on the clock and spent enormous energy navigating unfamiliar waters—wasted energy that may well explain his blunder in Game 6.

He certainly seemed exuberant after his win in the first game, in which he seemed to delay any tactical interchange for many moves—an attempt to avoid book and make use of the "horizon effect" Achilles' heel?

Garry was indeed in high spirits after winning Game 1 with 1. d3, an anti-computer strategy designed to dump Deep Blue out of book from the get-go. He took his entire team out for a lobster dinner, apparently in celebration of a match victory that was a foregone conclusion. It was their last lobster dinner!

Then came Game 2, when Kasparov—the World Champion with the well-earned reputation as a never-give-up slugger—resigned in a drawn position! He never seemed the same player to me after this.

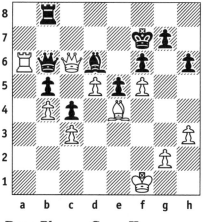

Deep Blue vs. Garry Kasparov, 1997, Game 2

Game 2 was a disaster. Garry answered Deep Blue's 1. e4 with the classical 1. ... e5, and met one of White's oldest and most respected opening plans, the Ruy López: 1. e4 e5 2. Nf3 Nc6 3. Bb5. The program played relentlessly, and for the most part accurately, reaching the position at right, in which Garry resigned. ▶

To the horror of Team Kasparov, later that evening our Fritz4 chess-playing program pointed out a definitive drawing line: 45. ...Qe3! 46. Qxd6 Re8! (preventing 47. Qc7+) 47. h4! (giving the White King an escape route to avoid a possible perpetual check) h5! (cutting off the escape)—drawn.

The World Champion had indeed resigned a drawn position! How could that happen? Later Kasparov explained that he had been so demoralized by the computer's relentless and human-like play to this point that he had "taken the computer's word" for the result.

Garry brooded over this result and obsessed over this move until he imagined himself faced with an unbeatable and virtually omniscient opponent, half-man and half-machine. The match continued, but the fun had gone out of it. Kasparov was visibly shaken. *He had begun to fear the computer.*

From this point forward in the match, Garry Kasparov became Everyman in front of his electronic Nemesis. My favorite cartoon about the match shows Garry hunched over his VCR with an arbiter holding a sign reading, "Kasparov vs. his VCR: Match–VCR." His nerves were frayed, the possibility of losing the match loomed, and he began to tire under the strain of six high-pressure games in a week. He was unable to capitalize on good positions in Games 3, 4 and 5. In Game 6, he snapped.

Well, something strange certainly happened in Game 6. After all, the match was still a tie going into this critical game. And Kasparov played known mistakes early in the game!

Yep, a visibly drained Kasparov stepped onstage for the final game, the match on the line. He played his second Caro-Kann Defense (1. e2-e4 c7-c6) of the match, a line he hasn't played against humans since he was a teenager.

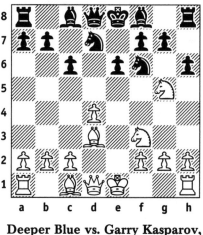

Deeper Blue vs. Garry Kasparov, 1997, Game 6

1. e2-e4 c7-c6 2. d2-d4 d7-d5 3. Nb1-c3 d5xe4 4. Nc3xe4 Nb8-d7 5. Ne4-g5 Ng8-f6 6. Bf1-d3 e7-e6 7. Ng1-f3 h7-h6?

Lost and still in book, a situation familiar to many of us play-at-home warriors. The correct move order is 7. ... Bf8-d6 8. Qd1-e2 h7-h6 9. Ng5-e4 Nf6xe4 10. Qe2xe4 Nd7-f6, when White retains his usual slight advantage.

8. Ng5xe6!
A known killer. Garry is playing a relatively unfamiliar opening, and he simply transposes moves, inadvertently playing ... h7-h6 before ... Bf8-d6. We've all made this kind of mistake against our computers at home—we just press the take-back or re-start button. But onstage with hundreds of thousands of dollars on the line and millions of people watching, Garry was caught like a deer in head-lights. He must have known instantly that he was dead. Deep Blue hadn't even broken a sweat. The original game (Wolff-Granda Zúniga, 1992) was in its database:

8. ... Qd8-e7 9. 0-0 f7xe6 10. Bd3-g6+ Ke8-d8 11. Bc1-f4 b7-b5? ▶

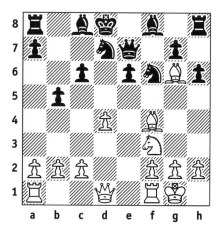

Garry's first move out of book, and it's a lemon. Still, other moves just prolong the agony.

12. a2-a4! Bf8-b7 13. Rf1-e1 Nf6-d5 14. Bf4-g3 Kd8-c8 15. a4xb5 c6xb5 16. Qd1-d3 Bb7-c6?

Better is 16. ...Qe7-b4, but not much better.

17. Bg6-f5 e6xf5 18. Re1xe7 Bf8xe7 19. c2-c4, resigns

Match to Deep Blue, 3.5-2.5. A remarkable and historic accomplishment—but don't kid yourself: If you think beating Deep Blue is hard, try beating Garry!

Look, here's what's especially strange to me. You emphasize Garry's unfamiliarity with the opening, but he played six championship matches against FIDE (International Chess Federation) Champion Anatoly Karpov, who relies heavily on Caro Kann. What gives here? It seems inconceivable that Garry could make these blunders!

The score of this match going into the last round could have easily been 4-1 in Garry's favor. That's how much better his chess was than Deep Blue's. Garry lost this game and the match like a human being. He underestimated, then overestimated the computer. He saw ghosts, he tired, he collapsed under the physical and emotional strain.

Deep Blue, on the other hand, won like a computer. It made moves, it took advantage of Garry's mistakes, it defended tough positions without flinching. It imagined nothing, and it lost no sleep over the possibility of losing the match.

What's the significance of this match—to humans?

The first lesson to learn from this match is an important one. When you sit down to play against a computer, your worst enemy is *you.* Grandmaster Savielly Tartakover is reported to have said, "The winner of a chess game is the player who makes the second-to-last blunder." Computers don't blunder–draw your own conclusion.

To win against a computer, your first step is to convince yourself that your machine is beatable. Remember that you're *losing* more games than the computer is *winning*. The next step is to weed blunders out of your repertoire. Often a human player will blunder a blown game back to you; a computer almost never does.

The next thing to remember is that the goal is not to beat the computer, but to improve your chess. In a match like Garry's, with $700,000 on the line for first place, you might not have that luxury. But at home with no one watching and no prize money at stake, your chess-playing computer is not an opponent–it's a training partner.

Good point. Once off the Mount Olympus of both human and computer play and into the average home, chess computers needn't be a threat of any kind!

Ten years ago, the only way to improve your chess radically was to hire a chess coach or to suffer repeated beatings in official chess tournaments against strong players. Both of these are still viable options, but today you can become a very strong player without ever sitting across the table from another human being–with your chess-playing computer. The trick is absolutely not to be intimidated by your computer. Challenge it. Force it to beat you by learning not to beat yourself.

And some commercially available computers these days even have special features that help you learn the openings–like the ones that Grandmaster Benjamin and you put into Deeper Blue.

Right. Don't be afraid to play book lines. They are "book lines" because they've been tested in real-life play and proven themselves effective. Study them. When you lose, assume you're the problem until you've reviewed your play and can't find any mistakes to blame the loss on.

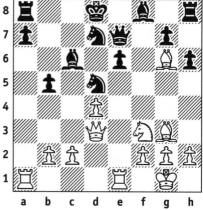

Well, that won't be very often!

And don't just *play* games. Review them, study them, think about them. Use your computer to study them. Figure out what you did wrong, try to correct your mistakes. Learn from them.

Finally, don't expect any easy wins. Against a computer, be prepared to fight to the last piece. Computers don't get demoralized in a bad position, and if your attention slips, theirs doesn't. They will be happy to nail you to the wall a Queen up or a Queen down!

And go easy on yourself! Garry is the best player in the world, maybe the best ever, and he broke every one of these rules in his match with Deep Blue. If he hadn't, I'm pretty sure Deeper Blue would still be fishing for the ultimate chess trophy!

Great advice, Don. Thank you for the insider's perspective on what will be, quite wrongly, looked back on for centuries as the event that showed computers to be smarter than humans. Keep the faith!

> *The mistakes are all there, waiting to be played.*
> *—Savielly Tartakover*

*Your only task in the opening is to
reach a playable middlegame!*
–Grandmaster Lajos Portisch

CHAPTER SIX

Openings—How to Pick
a Fight with Your Computer

Warning! We're now in the phase of the game that computers can play very, very well: the opening. But we're still not willing to concede even this stage of the game to our bloodless partners. For although the computers play from faultless memory—until they are out of their "book"—they are playing by rote.

The opening in chess refers to the first moves of the game, when both sides bring their pieces out. On a high level of human play, openings are memorized for up to 30 full moves (both White's and Black's half of each move). Top-level players have their favorite openings in their heads, and spend many hours re-memorizing them and keeping up on the latest innovations revealed in the games of the masters. But chess computers come with huge opening "books"—opening variations stored in the microchips in the case of stand-alone computers, or stored in the databases in the case of software programs for your PC. One of the inexpensive stand-alones we have on our desk now has 13,000 opening moves at its nearly instantaneous recall. ChessMaster 5000, the popular software program, offers 2,000 separate, named opening variations, and 27,000 *games*, not just moves, in its database. Of course, chess specialty software like ChessBase offers combinable packages of data that can literally take you to millions of games. And Fritz, the ChessBase playing program, can work in conjunction with such a database. Such technology is not as expensive as you might think.

The good news *again* is that even humans who don't have a skull full of subvariations can do very well in the opening by following some general principles. Remember that the opening is one of the three phases of the game, and each of these phases has unique guiding principles. So, keep in mind that these guidelines may apply to the other phases of the game as well, but not necessarily.

First of all, a player must try to control, or at least stake his claim to the board's "high ground"—the center of the board. He who controls the center has a definite advantage in the opening. His opponent finds it very difficult to coordinate his pieces or to get an attack going.

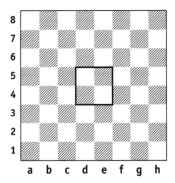

The central squares of e4, d4, e5, and d5 are the high ground of the chessboard. Occupy them!

In the opening, occupy as much of the center as possible, and exert as much control as possible over the center.

Another very clear rule of the opening is to get your *minor pieces*—Bishops and Knights—off your back rank and into the game as quickly as possible. Certainly your King must stay back in the opening. If fact, he should stay home until the endgame, when it's safe for him to come out. The only pieces that can get off the back rank without moving pawns out of their way are the Knights, of course, with their equestrian ability to jump. Your pieces and pawns must therefore work together quickly and accurately in the opening so that your opponent doesn't get an advantage.

Get your pieces off the back rank—"out of the box," as chess players say—and into positions that bear down on the center.

Take a look at this position, the quickest mate possible in chess. It's called "Fool's Mate" for obvious reasons. Some books say that no one really ever gets to play this sequence of moves in a real game. Not true! Co-author Al won a game in a St. Louis café that went:

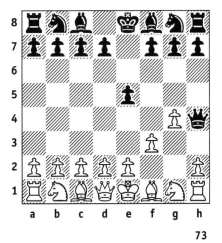

1. f2-f3   e7-e5
2. g2-g4??   Qd8-h4 mate!

But don't get your hopes up too high. Your computer will not fall for this. But the sequence does illustrate how quickly bad things can happen to violators of the opening rules.

Let's put the first two boxed rules together. Do you have a suggestion about the best first move for White? He has all the choices. Quickly, cover the smaller diagrams just below, and study the larger diagram at right, showing the pieces in their original positions. Select a move that occupies and controls the center, and at the same time opens a gate for backrank pieces.

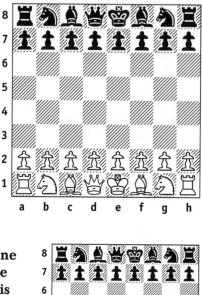

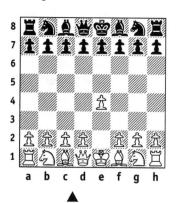

Either one of these moves is the "best" because they both adhere to the above rules.

▲

This move occupies e4, and attacks d5 and f5. So it certainly does its share of center duty. Additionally, it opens the d1-h5 diagonal for the White Queen, and the f1-a6 diagonal for the White Bishop. We'd say it satisfies our first two principles of the opening perfectly. In fact that's the whole point. You can't do better on the first move. Your computer, despite its thousands of opening moves to call on, will often make this move—just like you.

▲

This move occupies d4, and attacks c5 and e5. It opens the diagonal c1-h6 for White's Queen Bishop. It gives the Queen two moves of breathing space on the d-file. It meets our two principles perfectly. Advocates of this move like to point out that the d-pawn is supported—by the Queen. The move 1. e2-e4 opens a few more squares for those behind it, but it is out there on its own, and will require support.

And there's a general truth about each. Those who thrive on sharp *tactics*, the short-term thrust, prefer 1. e2-e4, while those who prefer *strategy*, long-range thinking, gravitate toward 1. d2-d4. There's a poetic logic to it. The pawn daring enough to step out there into the spotlight leads the way to riskier play. The pawn who steps out to the same important center, but with a lifeline of sorts, leads the game down a bit quieter path. There are many exceptions to this generalization, but it remains a valid rule of thumb.

By the way, you noticed, we're sure, that you found the perfect first move in the complicated game of chess with just two general principles and your own human logic. (We *love* making this point! It should make you feel good too.)

There are other first moves used by modern masters. As in any discipline—art, science, or sport—there are modernists who dream up plans counter to the "classically" accepted theories just because that's human nature. The most important modernist concept for Black is to let White claim a big center, and then to attack it. Usually, this entails *"fianchettoing"* a Bishop—usually Black's King's Bishop. Until the 1920s this type of development was deemed eccentric. (The term comes from the Italian *fiancata,* "playing to the flank.") *Fianchettoed* Bishops look like this. ▶

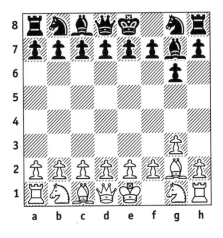

Fianchettoed Bishops are developed on the long diagonals, to exert a force on the center and beyond. A player can fianchetto one or both of his Bishops, but a double fianchetto requires a subtle sense of strategy.

Keep this pattern in mind for later. Right now, remember that giving up the center without a fight is usually a terrible idea. Even ceding its occupation to your opponent in the hope of attacking it requires a deep and subtle understanding of the process, and often turns out badly even for those who are knowledgeable. We simply want to alert you that these and other opening ideas exist in master chess: You'll see them in books and magazines. Think of them for now as a sort of behind-the-back dribble that a basketball coach would like you to keep for games in the driveway against a younger—and much shorter—brother.

Let's look at some more guiding principles of the opening. Chess players talk about *development.* Development is bringing your pieces off their home squares and into play.

> **Develop, develop, develop! An army never won a battle by staying home!**

Okay, so this rule tells you to bring them out. But to which squares, and in what order?

We need to refine this rule. But it's so important, we wanted it to stand alone for emphasis. Let's add these Ten Commandments of Development to help us find the right first moves for our pieces. We all do better to emphasize the positive. There are eight "do's" and two "don'ts." All these "rules" have exceptions, of course, and if you see a strong move that breaks these commandments, then make it! But they'll be right most of the time.

Ten Commandments of Development

1. Develop your pieces so that they exert force on the center—that is, put them in a position from which they support your own center pawn, or they control a center square, or they attack an enemy pawn in the center. Your pieces themselves don't often belong on one of the four center squares, because they're too easily attacked by the less valuable pawns.
2. Develop at least one Knight before you develop your Bishops.
3. Develop your kingside pieces first, since you'll probably castle in that direction.
4. Develop minor pieces—Knights and Bishops—before your Queen and Rooks.
5. Castle early—it gets your King into safety and develops your Rook toward the center—all in one move.
6. Unless there's a really compelling reason, move each piece just once in the opening. The idea is to get them all into play before starting a major operation. Don't attack with just a piece or two. Such a premature attack in the opening would be a waste of time, likely to leave you in the worse position, unless your opponent has made bad mistakes of his own.
7. Wait to move your Queen until you know where such heavy artillery belongs.
8. Be careful when moving any pawns around your King. You could

give your opponent a fatal path to your Monarch. Recall the two-move "Fool's Mate."

9. Don't move your Rook pawns, especially to try to free your Rooks. Rooks should first come to the center along your back rank, where they are likely to exert pressure on *files*. In the opening, Rooks should be treated like heavy artillery. Keep them in back of the action, where they will have their effect, and won't likely be captured.

10. Don't make more than one or two pawn moves in the opening in normal circumstances. After that, develop your pieces!

As always, before you move a piece to a square, take a careful look to see if the square is attacked by an enemy piece. Refer to the point chart on page 55. Don't let your opponent exchange a less valuable piece for a more valuable piece unless you have a very, very good reason.

A diagram is worth a thousand words

Supposing you didn't have to worry about what your computer was going to move, what would the ideal opening look like? It would have to look very much like the position at right.

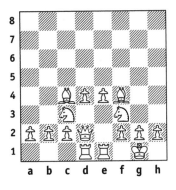

Remember this picture. White has occupied the center with his King and Queen pawns, and moved every other piece to bear on the center. You can calculate that he has moved every piece once, except for the King's Rook, which castled and then moved to e1. The Knights are a short-stepping piece, as we've noticed in other stages of the game. It's worth drawing attention to a special guideline about them.

Normally, the best places for the Knights are f3, c3, f6, and c6. Here they put pressure on the center.

Okay, so we've been shadow boxing, working on our punches without having to worry about an opponent. Let's give him—it—some thought. We know that it will play well. What general strategies can increase our chances of beating a non-human opponent? Asking this question takes us straight into the realm of first-class chess considerations. Although openings have their own guiding principles, they serve no purpose in themselves.

> **An opening well played on both sides serves only to take the players into a middlegame. One can feel he or she "won" the opening by getting into a middlegame that feels good.**

So what kind of a middlegame do we want against our computer? Well, we've already learned that our computer's susceptibility to the *horizon effect* makes it hard for it to properly foresee the formidable dangers of a *pawn storm*. To launch a *pawn storm* against the castled enemy King, you must push a squadron of pawns from the same side of the board. Obviously, you don't want to weaken the pawn defenses in front of your own King by doing this.

This advice is especially good against computers. Against other humans, be careful of castling queenside with the Black pieces. It's dangerous, given White's head start of the first move. Castling kingside (or *castling short*) is almost always safer than *castling long*.

Remember, to launch a successful pawn storm, you normally need to have achieved a very stable center—preferably one that's locked up, and doesn't permit your computer to counterattack there, which is the classic antidote to the attack on the wing. So, if you can castle on the opposite wing as your computer opponent and lock up the center, do so. Then, after you're fully developed (with the exception of the Rook behind your storming pawns; leave that one where it is), start that *pawn storm.*

Castling on the opposite side from your computer's King prepares you to launch a *pawn storm*, an attack that can take advantage of the *horizon effect*.

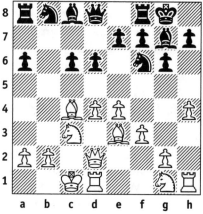

Now, back to *fianchettoed* Bishops. If your computer castles behind such a Bishop, give it chances early in the game to trade it off, because many computers will double your pawns whenever possible. Practically whenever they can trade off a piece of equal value and double your pawns, they will. Your computer may not understand that when it trades away the Bishop *fianchettoed* in front of its King, it weakens—perhaps fatally—a complex of squares crucial to the monarch's defense.

White just played 6. Nb1-c3 to tempt his computer opponent to play 6. ... Bg7xc3. White's c-pawns will be doubled. But the dark squares around Black's King will be seriously weakened—a much more serious problem.

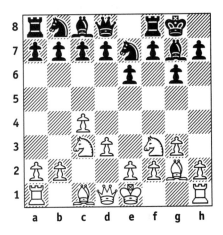

Some computers and software offer features that help you learn standard book openings. Once you learn a few of these, there's another trick you can try to throw your computer off its electronic feed in what is normally its strongest territory.

If you can play a sound move, one that follows our opening principles, and take your computer out of its "book," play it! Your computer will immediately lose one of its big advantages: its perfect memory.

Of course, you want to make sure the move has no immediate drawbacks. But you'll be surprised how often you can get out of book without making a bad move. Your computer will then be thrown on its own resources. It will have to "think" for itself, rather than simply remember moves. And computers sometimes aren't given much in the way of thoughts about openings, since they're given such big libraries of specific moves. When they are forced to decide for themselves, they sometimes make moves based on middlegame principles instead of opening principles, and you'll get an advantage.

The *horizon effect* can be really killing in the opening. There are so many possibilities that the computer, number-crunching instead of simply recalling, can make some pretty silly mistakes.

White has intentionally stayed away from a book position, throwing the computer on its own in the opening. It errs immediately!

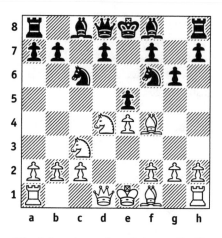

Black has just played 1. ... e7-e5?

Steven Cisneros vs. ChessMaster 4000, 1995

1.	...	e7-e5?
2.	Nd4xc6	d7xc6
3.	Qd1xd8+	Ke8xd8
4.	Bf4xe5	

White has an extra pawn and a won position early in the game. ChessMaster, a program that has a perfect memory of thousands of opening positions, found itself in unfamiliar seas and foundered quickly. There were just too many possibilities for a search unguided by sound principles.

None of this means that you should make truly bad moves to get out of the book. Always double check to make sure that the square you're about to move a piece to is not attacked by a unit of less value. And look after the safety of your King!

Show me three variations in the leading handbook on the openings, and I will show you two of those three that are defective.
—Emanuel Lasker, World Champion for
27 consecutive years

Chess is 99% tactics.
–Richard Teichmann

CHAPTER SEVEN

Middlegame, Part I: Tactics— The Dirty Dozen of Chess

Once your pieces are developed, which generally takes ten to fifteen moves, you're out of opening and into the middlegame. No amount of memorizing moves will help. Mathematician Claude Shannon has calculated that there are more possible chess moves than atoms in the universe!

When you've been in this stage of the game, you've perhaps felt that it was difficult to know what you should be thinking about–exactly what the priorities are. That's an instinctively good reaction! You need some guiding principles, and you won't be surprised at this point to know that we have some for you, in this chapter and the next, that will help you to win in the middlegame.

Let's go to the video tape!

In this chapter, we'll look at a lot of positions: "freeze frames" of actual chess games between international chess stars. Their ideas live on in these games. We won't look at whole games (although that, too, is a terrific way to improve), just the positions that ended the contest, to see tactics in action!

Tactics are the real hammer and nails of chess. Look at the diagrams carefully and try to predict the move to come. It will be confusing at first, but you'll soon get the hang of it–and it's chess *play*, after all, not work! Remember, you can set up these positions on your own computer and try different lines of play against it to test the truth of these positions. You'll learn things that will stick with you–and your opponents–for the rest of your life.

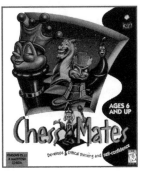

> **In the opening: the armies draw up the battle lines. In the middlegame: the battle—with all its grand strategies, side skirmishes, and individual heroics—is in full swing.**

The middlegame is overwhelmingly the source of victory or defeat. It can be the most confusing stage of a chess game because it's the most complicated. All the pieces are in play, the bullets are flying. To avoid disaster, one has to keep his head in more ways than one. So we'd better have some more guiding principles and other shortcuts to navigate this universe of possibilities. We do.

> **To play the middlegame, chess players rely on two basic thinking tools:**
> > ✓ **Strategy, or planning**
> > ✓ **Tactics**

Strategy—the term chess players like to call the plan for the game—is the subject of the next chapter on the middlegame (Part II). But first we're going to show you some common tactics, or tricks of the trade. After all, before you can execute a game plan, you have to be able to block, kick and pass!

> **Your King's safety is ultimate. Don't forget about His Majesty in the heat of battle. Whether you're considering tactics or planning, whether you're attacking or defending, you should check your King's safety!**

Richard Teichmann, one of the great attacking players of the game, said that chess is ninety-nine percent tactics. He's right in a very important way. You can have the greatest plan in the world, but if you keep falling into traps and tricks, you'll never get a chance to try out your plan. Moreover, the building blocks for enacting your plan are tactics! Chess players have a name for the series of forcing moves that lead to an improved position for one player: a *combination.*

Computers and tactics in the middlegame

Computers, despite their lack of a "book" to rely on for the middlegame, do very well at *tactics*. All of our units excelled at finding these forced series of moves ending in mate or the winning of significant material. We set them at one minute per move for their work throughout this chapter.

Computers do not do as well at *planning*. We'll discuss their problems with strategy in the next chapter. Don't despair! Keep in mind that to have winning combinations at your disposal in a real game, you have to plan well.

> **Most often, we get things done on the chess board by using tactics, or the *threat* of tactics.**

Let's look at the basic thrusts and parries of chess's mental swordfighting: the Dirty Dozen. We'll explain them as if you're executing them against your opponent. That will be less confusing, and more enjoyable to think about!

> **Practicing these 12 basic types of tactics will vault your game to a new level. You'll smash players–human and inhuman–you previously struggled with!**

Tactic #1: decoy

Decoys do just what their name implies. They're used to force an enemy piece to a particular square. This tactical device can be very handy–especially when used in conjunction with other tactics.

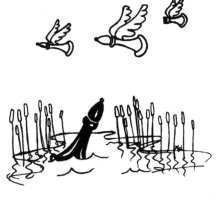

Take a look at the classic of decoying that follows. Think about what you like and don't like about the position for each side. (This is the kind of *analysis* chess players do to determine what may be a good plan to follow.) Take two important concepts and apply them to the snapshot at right. How would you evaluate each side in relation to *development* and *King safety*?

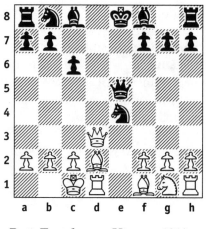

Although White's *kingside* is completely at home in this late-opening position, his queenside pieces exert a powerful influence on the center. His Rook, already on d1 while Black's are still stuck in the corners, exerts latent power down the open d-file. Black's King is woefully located on one of two adjacent, open files at the other end, looking rather like a bowling pin at the end of a well-used lane. Certainly, Black, if given time, could develop his f8-Bishop to e7 and castle into safety. White has an advantage. He should heed Steinitz's admonition to act now or expect his advantage to evaporate.

Reti–Tartakover, Vienna, 1910
White to move

We gave Battle Chess 4000 a chance to show its stuff, and it did, announcing *mate in three* immediately and playing the moves out instantly.

Battle Chess 4000 vs. Alan

1. Qd3-d8+!!
This is the decoy. Black must certainly take the Queen, moving to d8.

1.   Ke8xd8
2. Bd2-g5++
A *discovered check* that is also a *double check*. Such a move is the nuclear bomb of the chessboard.

2. ...   Kd8-c7
Or 2. ... Ke8 3. Rd8, checkmate!

3. Bg5-d8 checkmate ▶
All of Black's pieces, except his King, are unmoved from the original position. It's as if they can only

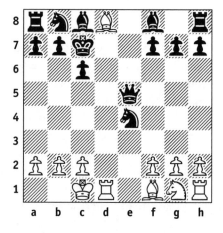

watch, frozen in humiliation. The decoy is the "one" in the old one-two.

Take a look at this snapshot from a game that was played when Calvin Coolidge was in the White House.

White has a Knight for two pawns. But the dominating factor in such a wide-open position with mutually unsafe Kings is who's on move. So it's not too surprising White has a devastating shot—in this case, a decoy.

A mid-range tabletop found this one instantly.

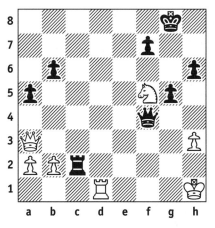

Vidmar–Euwe, Carlsbad, 1923
White to move

Mid-range tabletop vs. Alan

1. Qa3-f8+!!
Black must take the Queen, since the only other legal move available to him, 1. … Kg8-h8, allows Qf8-g7, checkmate.

1. … Kg8xf8
2. Rd1-d8 checkmate
The Knight cooperates nicely, penning the King in for the mate.

The next example of decoy in action comes from a more modern game. White sees a chance to defeat a future World Champion in a brilliant fashion, again using decoy. White has a dominating Queen in the center, a far-advanced pawn, and a Rook ready to claim the open g-file. In fact, g8 seems like a terribly weak square. Hmmm.

Battle Chess 4000 solved this one without a hiccup. ▶

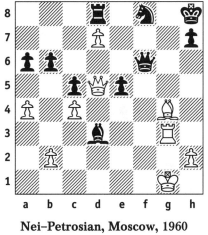

Nei–Petrosian, Moscow, 1960
White to move

Battle Chess 4000 vs. Alan

1. Qd5-g8+!
Black must capture with 1. … Kh8xg8, and White plays 2. Bg4-e6, *double check* and mate! Note how Black's Knight blocks his Rook from controlling the critical g8 square.

Tactic #2: the power of the pin!

The most common tactic is *pinning*. It occurs in nearly every game. It involves three chess pieces—two of your enemy's and one of yours—standing in a straight line, whether on a diagonal, file, or rank. You can *pin* your opponent's pieces with your Queen, Rook, or Bishop.

The White Queen pins the Black Rook to the Black King. It's an *absolute* pin—the Rook cannot legally move, because the King would be exposed to check.

The Black Bishop pins the White Knight to the White Queen. It's a *relative* pin because the Knight could legally move if White decides it's worth the cost!

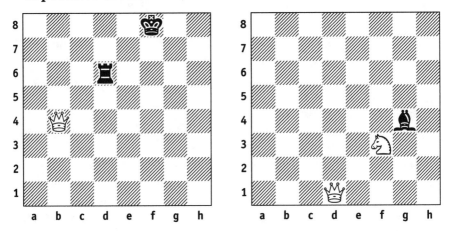

Notice that attacking the pinned piece with a pawn in any of these positions would win you material, even if it were the defender's move!

A pinned piece is often vulnerable because it is immobile. Chess players have a saying: "Pin it and win it!"

The White Rook pins the Black Queen to the Black King. The White Rook is protected by its partner. White will win material!

Once a piece is pinned, look for ways to "pile up" on the immobilized piece. Since it can't move, you can sometimes attack it more times than it can be defended, and win the piece!

Let's take a look at some more complicated pins in middlegame action, and also challenge the computers to find the follow-ups. Once again, we're helped by our USCF master, Alan Kantor, who is artificially putting himself in losing positions game after game in our testing department. (He can hardly wait to get away and beat some humans!)

Notice, below, that Black has a pin on the White Knight on f3. But Black is badly lacking in *development*–always a tip-off that there may be a tactic or counter-tactic in the air. And very important–Black's pin is a *relative* pin. White can ignore it if he chooses!

Upscale tabletop (rated Master) vs. Alan

1. Nf3xe5!   Bg4xd1?
Just testing. Better was 1. ... d6xe5, keeping his losses down to one pawn.

2. Bc4xf7+   Ke8-e7
3. Nc3-d5 checkmate

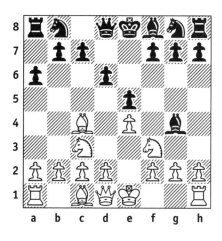

This is actually a well-known opening trap, "Legal's Mate." The computer found it all nearly instantly. It shows how a *relative* pin can sometimes be broken with great effect!

We set up this next position on a mid-range tabletop model. It found the winning move. ▶

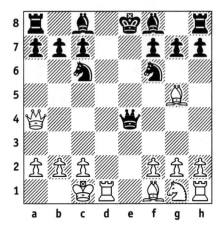

Mid-range tabletop vs. Alan

1. Rd1-d8+!!   Ke8xd8

The Black King has been *decoyed*– the White Bishop on g5 now holds the Black Knight on f6 in an *absolute pin*. And what was this Knight protecting before it was pinned?

2. Bg5xf6+

Also good is Qxe4.

2. ...   Qe4-e7
3. Bf6xe7+   Bf8xe7

So, White has won material, and should win the game.

In this next game, Black is a pawn ahead, but his Rook is trapped out of play. He is, in effect, a Rook down until he gets this artillery into the game. Steinitz said that you must strike when you have such an advantage, or risk losing it! So White looks for the winning tactic, and finds a diabolical use of the pin!

We set this up on a master-rated tabletop, and it found the move quickly!

Master-level tabletop vs. Alan

1. Qe3-a3+!   Qe6-e7
2. Be4-c6!

Beautiful, imaginative, and quite logical, based on the pinning motif and Black's *de facto* material deficit! Black's Queen is *pinned* by the White Queen, so Black can't cap-

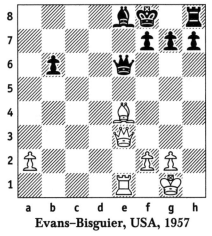

Evans–Bisguier, USA, 1957

ture the White's Rook that will either snatch Black's Queen or, if it moves, take the Bishop with checkmate!

We should note that Alan knew Black could have put up stiffer resistance on move one by playing 1. ... Kg8, but then the game would continue with 2. Be4xh7+! (*discovered attack*) Kg8xh7 3. Re1xe6, and White's Queen will easily beat Black's uncoordinated pieces.

Tactic #3: cross-pins aren't really in a bad mood

The next game snapshot is another example of *pin-breaking*, but this time it's done with another type of pin, called a *cross-pin*.

A medium priced tabletop found this whole line of play instantly!

Mid-range tabletop vs. Alan

1. Bd4-c5
This looks painful! Black's Queen is pinned to his King by a lowly but supported Bishop, who threatens to capture it! But the White King is also exposed, along the same diagonal his Bishop stands on. And Black has a dark-squared Bishop of his own. Hmmm.

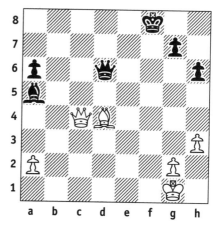

1. ...   Ba5-b6!
The *cross-pin.* It seems to get Black out of his mess. The White Bishop can't take the Black Queen. On 2. Bc5xb6, White simply plays 2. ... Qd6xb6+, with an even game. Are the tactics extinguished?

2.   Qc4-f4+!
No! This charming move is the final blow! White's Queen checks, and *piles up* on the pinned Black Queen

Pins can be simple or complex. Pin your opponent's men to his other pieces of greater value. It reduces their effectiveness—and makes him sweat! Okay, that last part applies only to your *human* opponents.

> **Wilhelm Steinitz, the founder of modern strategy, pointed out that if you had an advantage, you had the *obligation* to attack, or your advantage would evaporate.**

Tactic #4: deflection

Deflection is the other side of the *decoy* coin. Both tactics move the enemy pieces. While *decoy* moves an enemy piece *to* a certain square, *deflection* removes it *from* a particular square. Here's a simple example, which Fritz found easily. ▶

White's only chance of winning rests in queening his far-advanced d-pawn. But the Black Rook is already positioned behind it, keeping White's own Rook from supporting his pawn. White has a move that *deflects* the Black Rook from crucial guard duty.

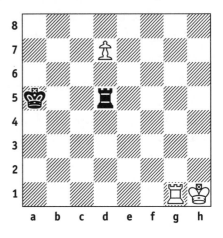

1. Rd5-g5!
This move actually *pins* the Black Rook to his King so the pawn can advance. Since the Rook is unprotected, Black takes it.

1. ...   Rd5xg5
2. d7-d8 (Q)+
White would win with a Queen against Rook, but here he does even better. He queens with a *double attack* (see below) on White's King and Rook. He wins the Rook!

Tactic #5: double attacks

A *double attack* is a single move that makes two separate threats at the same time, as White did on his second move in the example immediately above.

For the more complicated test to the right, we went back to our wise-cracking, middle-range tabletop.

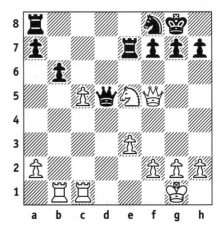

Krogius–Sergiyevsky,
19th Russian Championship
White to move

Mid-range tabletop vs. Alan

1. Ne5-g6!!
With one move, White threatens both Black's Rook (with the White Knight) and Queen (with the White Queen). Black could resign after this shot. If he moves his Queen, White wins the exchange with Ng6xe7.

2. ...   Re7-d7
Black moves his Rook away from the threat and supports his Queen, defending against both threats. But now White has another *double attack*.

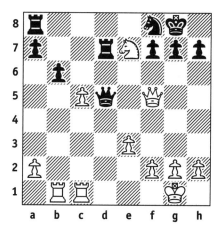

2. Ng6-e7+!   ▶
The Knight simultaneously attacks Black's King and Queen. (When one piece performs a double attack, it's often called a *fork*.) If Black takes the Knight with his Rook, then his Queen falls to Qf5xd5.

Tactic #6: back-rank mates

Technically, back-rank mates are not a tactic, but a theme based on an all-too-common weakness. But they come up a lot, and you can win many, many games by keeping your eyes open for this weakness, and pounce when you see it. And of course, avoid the weakness yourself.

The basic idea is shown below. Black's King is checkmated because he has no lateral protection and his own pawns pen him in. One check from a lone Rook or Queen, and it's time to press the "New Game" key.

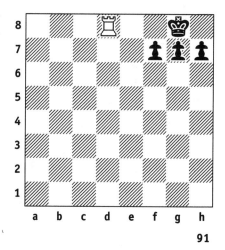

> **So when the pawns in front of either castled King are unmoved, and Rooks or Queens are on the board, watch out for the back-rank mate!**

Here's a position that will show you the way that back-rank mates can develop unexpectedly—unless you're looking out for them. We let the master-level tabletop handle this problem, which it was instantly happy to do. Take a look for yourself before reading the solution. And don't be afraid to "sacrifice"— to invest a piece of great value to achieve the goal!

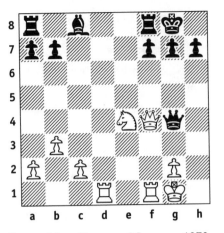

Master-rated tabletop vs. Alan

Lemachko–Popova, Moscow, 1970

1.	Qf4xf7+!	Rf8xf7
2.	Rd1-d8+	Rf7-f8
3.	Rd8xf8, checkmate	

The greater the value of the piece, the more startling the sacrifice. We wanted to see if one of our mid-range tabletops could find this stunning idea. It did, but it thought first for two and a half minutes! (It was set to complete 60 moves in 60 minutes and used its discretion to spend extra time here.)

Mid-range tabletop vs. Alan

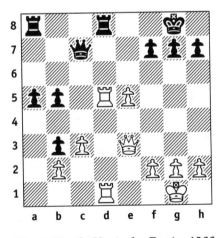

1. Qe3-a7!!

The Queen is poison. If Black captures it with either his own Queen or Rook, one of these pieces are *deflected* from their duties of guarding the *back rank*, and White mates, starting with 2. Rd5xd8+. This idea of "you can't touch me whatever I do" is especially amusing when the valuable Queen herself is the immune piece.

Minic–Honfi, Vrnjacka Banja, 1966
White to move

1.	...	Qc7-c8
2.	Qa7xa8	

The Queen has found a winning idea, and won't give up!

2.	...	Qc8xa8

3. Rd4xd8+ Qa8xd8
4. Rd1xd8 checkmate

Tactic #7: the skewer—the *shish kebab* of chess

If the pin is one side of the coin, the skewer is the opposite side. Both are straight-line tactics. In a pin, a less valuable piece shelters a more valuable piece from an attack. With a *skewer,* the more valuable piece is attacked, forced to move, and exposes a less valuable piece to capture.

Here's a composed example of a powerful *skewer*. A master-rated tabletop found it in a microchip second. Try it yourself before looking at the answer. Guide your thinking by remembering that a *skewer* attacks a more valuable enemy piece that is in a straight line with a less valuable piece behind it. It's a bit like sticking a cooking skewer through a line-up of delicacies for the grill!

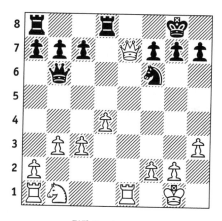

White to move

Master-level tabletop vs. Alan

1. ...   Rd8-e8!
White's Queen must avoid capture by moving, and exposes the Rook behind it to Black's Rook on e8. Notice here that Black could play his skewering move because his well-placed Knight adds additional protection to e8. If the horseman were off on a ride, ignoring its King, and *not* protecting e8, White would have a *back-rank mate* after 1. ... Rd8-e8. Do you see it? It starts with 2. Qxe8+.

Tactic #8: blocking

Blocking (sometimes called "*obstruction*") is a tactical device that limits the mobility of the enemy in some specific, critical way. Most of the time, the enemy King is the target. The *smothered mate* in Chapter 2–where Black's King was surrounded by his own men, blocked from even a single legal move–is an extreme example of *blocking*. Usually the block is achieved through a series of *forcing* checks. Take a look at this example. Material is balanced, but White's pieces are menacing Black's *cornered* King, and it's White's move. We gave Fritz a shot, and it took it in a non-heartbeat.

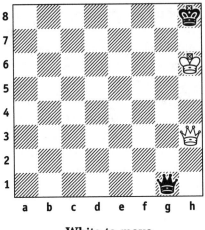

White to move

Fritz vs. Alan

1. Qh3-c8+   Qg8
The *block* has been executed. Now the Black King has no *escape* squares.

2. Qc8-c3+   Qg8-g7+
3. Qc3xg7 checkmate ▶
Here is the final position. Look familiar? It's our Queen mate, from Chapter 2! The goal has been reached by *tactics*–an extremely common occurrence!

Blocking problems can test your imagination–and that can improve your chess! This next one is a mate-in-three (next page) that we tried on our middle-of-the-road tabletop. Take a few minutes to try to solve the position before seeing how two different computers played. Don't be afraid to sacrifice big material to achieve the goal!

We set up this one on our mid-level model that always has something to "say." We didn't use its problem-solving mode, in which a search can be done for mate in a specific number of moves, but stuck to a 60-moves-in-60-minutes tournament level. It didn't find the shortest win, but it did find a sure win, very quickly. As a practical matter, this is hard to argue with.

Mid-range tabletop vs. Alan

1. Qg1-g4+
A Queen up, our little plastic partner has found a winning idea. But he didn't find mate in three. ▼

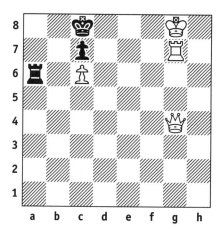

White to move;
he has mate in three

1. ...   Kc8-b8
If 1. ... Kc8-d8, then 2. Qg4-d7, checkmate. So Black's first move was *forced.*

2. Qg4-d7   Kb8-a7 ▶
Now it's a straight-ahead, bullying mate in two.

3. Qd7xc7+   Ka7-a8
4. Qc7-b7 mate
So our tabletop computer won without using the *blocking* tactic

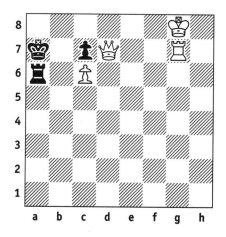

We tried the same problem out on ChessMaster 5000, set for solving a mate in three. Look back to the diagram at the top of this page. Reread the hints in the blocking paragraph on the facing page while ChessMaster is thinking. Whoops! Time's up!

ChessMaster 5000 vs. Alan

1. Qg1-a7!

The Queen is *sacrificed* to *decoy* the Black Rook to a square on which it *blocks* its own King. Three tactics in one move! Black must capture the Queen because it threatens both *checkmate* and capturing the Rook.

1.	...	Ra6xa7
2.	Kg8-f7	

A so-called "quiet" move. The King steps out of the way of his last piece. But, because of the *block*, Black can't stop the mating threat!

2.	...	Ra7-a1 (or any other move)
3.	Rg7-g8 checkmate ▶	

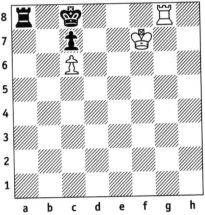

Tactic #9: discovered attack

This tactic is well named. You move one of your pieces—with a check, mate threat, or some other forceful move—and in so doing uncover another of your pieces lurking behind it. This uncovered piece attacks the enemy in a different point. Here's a position from one of former World Champion Bobby Fischer's games, when he was still a teenager. His opponent takes a pawn, and falls into a discovered attack that ends the game, adding him to the long list of the American genius's chess victims.

A master-level tabletop stood in for Bobby, and found the *discovery* in a few seconds.

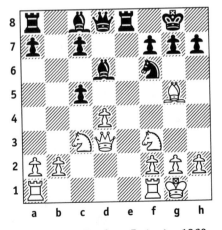

Ghitescu–Fischer, Leipzig, 1960
White to move and make a mistake (à la Tartakover)!

Alan vs. upscale (rated Master)

1.	d4xc5?	Bd6xh2+

The Bishop moves, and Black discovers the Black Queen is now menacing his own. But he has to deal with the check, of course!

2. Kg1xh2   Qd8xd3

White is a Queen down. Not a rosy prospect against Bobby! White resigned, of course.

At right is a nice example of *discovered attack* working with *decoy*. A mid-range stand-alone found it quickly.

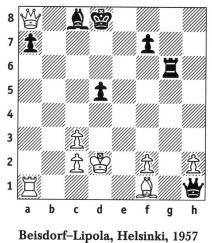

Beisdorf–Lipola, Helsinki, 1957
White to move

Mid-range tabletop vs. Alan

1. Qa8xc8+!   Kd8xc8

The King has been decoyed to c8. Now where's the *discovered attack*?

2. Bf1-h3+ !   resigns

There it is. The Bishop moves with check to reveal the White Rook on a1. Black must answer the check. Then White plays Ra1xh1. Since he *sacrificed* his own Queen for a Bishop on move one, White comes out a Bishop ahead!

Tactic #10: double check

The nuclear warheads of chess! Don't get in the way of one if you can help it. Double check is always a form of *discovered check*. One of your pieces moves, giving check, and at the same time uncovers another of your pieces that gives check as well.

Watch how Aaron Nimzovitch, who must have spent extra time standing on his head–his way to get blood to his brain–on this day almost 90 years ago, finds a game-stopper. By the way, our bloodless tabletop master found it quickly too.

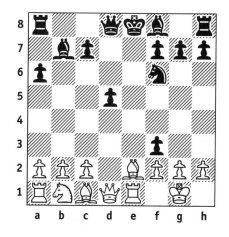

Nimzovitch–Rickhoff, Pernov, 1910
White to move

Upscale tabletop (rated Master) vs. Alan

1. Be2-b5++!! checkmate

The move gets two plusses because it gives two checks, and two exclamation points because it's a wonderful idea. Notice that the White Bishop on b5 is immune from capture because Black's King must move out of check from *both* the Bishop and Rook. It can't, poor surprised Monarch!

Tactic #11: in-between move

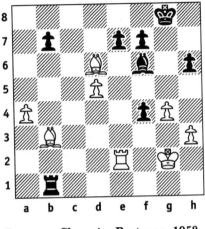

Rossetto–Sherwin, Portoroz, 1958
Black to move

This is the quintessential *surprise* move. The Germans have a dour-sounding word for it, *Zwischenzug* (pronounced TSVISH-un-tsook). Your opponent makes a move which he thinks forces a certain reply that's to his advantage. But you come up with a different move that turns the tables! Ah, *Schadenfreude!*

White has just played 1. Bb4xd6. He assumes Black must recapture with 1. … e7xd6 here to keep from losing material. But he has a surprise! Fritz found it in no time.

Alan vs. Karpov

1. ...   f4-f3+

The pawn steps forward to *double attack* White's King and Rook. It *decoys* the King to the third rank. Again, the tactics work in tandem to win.

2. Kf2xf3   Rb1xb3+

And only after White moves out of check, does Black play the expected … e6xd6, coming out a piece ahead!

All kinds of *in-between, surprise* moves are possible. When it looks as if you or your opponent is forced to make a certain move, look around. You never know, you may find a surprising use for one of the dirty dozen!

Tactic #12: overloading

If an overloaded piece could talk, it would probably tell you, "I've only got *no* hands!" When a piece has too many important duties, it's a weak point in the enemy's camp. Concentrate on it! You may be able to apply one of our other basic tactics to take advantage of its plight. Take a look at the Bishop in this composed position. A mid-range computer found this mate-in-two immediately.

Mid-range tabletop vs. Alan

1. Rb1-b8+!
The Bishop had to guard both b8 and f8. So White *decoys* it to one of these squares, and then hits the other!

1. ...   Bd6xb8
2. Rf1-f8 mate
When you play your own middlegames, be careful not to give one piece too many defensive

tasks. You've got a whole army—divide up your assignments fairly! When looking over your opponent's defensive position, keep an eye out for soldiers he's overtasked.

Use the "Dirty Dozen!"

The tactics we've looked at work in every phase of the game, but opportunities to use them abound in the middlegame, where many pieces are in play. Always be on the lookout for a good use of one of these Dirty Dozen. When you spot such a use, you'll probably see a way to get a winning advantage!

decoy	double attack	double check
pin	back-rank mate	in-between move
cross-pin	blocking	skewer
deflection	discovered attack	overloading

A game is always won through a mistake,
either the opponent's or one's own.
−Savielly Tartakover

It is better to sacrifice your opponent's men.
—Savielly Tartakover

CHAPTER EIGHT

Middlegame, Part II: Strategy—Even a Bad Plan Is Better Than No Plan!

In the last chapter you learned about the battle axes and short swords of the Royal Game. You're now capable of doing some dastardly deeds on the chessboard. But you also saw that computers are exceptionally strong at tactics. Chapter 4 was their forum to flex their chips. They can "see" every direct threat—for both sides—that isn't over their *horizons*.

But chess is a battle with a long-term goal. In a well-played game, even the short-term skirmishes are part of a plan. In short, each middle game is a different and complicated trip with a lot of turns. You need to make a road map. Computers aren't good at this kind of planning. It's simply beyond that famous *horizon*.

The paradox in all this is that, although chess players need a middle-game plan, even the greatest players change plans frequently, as the game progresses, because conditions change. For example, your plan may be to pile pieces against your opponent's King and play for a checkmating attack. Good plan! But while you're trying to execute this, your opponent calls every one of his pieces home to the defense of his King, leaving his pawns on the other side of the board without protection. You don't have an idea of how to proceed with your plan to checkmate. Should you change your plan to attack his now weakened pawns? Yes! Often, that's exactly how chess *is* played at the highest levels.

Planning is essential in chess. There are too many possibilities—a number greater than atoms in the universe—to see everything. Natur-

---

Don't be afraid to make a plan because it might not be the "best" one—you can always change it! But don't make moves without *some* plan! Confidence will come with experience.

---

ally, none of us will ever look at two billion chess positions (no matter how long we live and how much chess we play). But by knowing where we're going when we do play, we'll score hundreds of checkmates! This applies to all phases of the game.

General principles will help you plan. Running over the following checklist before each of your moves will raise your play to new levels.

Assess the existing position! Ask yourself the "Big Six" middlegame questions every time it's your move!

---

1. **Is my King safe? Is my opponent's?** Check to see if your opponent has more pieces around your King than you do. If he does, shift some pieces to your King's defense! Be especially careful with your Knights. If you need one or more to guard your King, remember that these short-hoppers can't travel fast, so keep them close.

   When playing your computer, you'll find that build-ups, bringing your pieces in the proximity of his King, ready for a breakthrough, will often pay dividends. The computer will bump into its *horizon* effect, and may not "see" the danger of your build-up in time to take defensive actions. If you have an overwhelming attacking position, you must "use it or lose it"! Your advantage can evaporate quickly.

2. **What is my opponent threatening?** Pay special attention to his last move. Does it attack anything? In the last chapter, you saw how good computers are at tactics. Watch out for the Dirty Dozen!

3. **Are my own pieces well protected? Are my opponent's?** Don't leave your pieces strewn around the board unprotected. Chess players refer to such pieces as *loose*, or *en prise*. They make it too easy for your opponent to win them through the use of the *double attack* or other tactics. If you see that your opponent's pieces are loose, start looking for a tactical shot based on this weakness!

4. **Do I have individual pieces that aren't contributing, or worse, is my whole position "cramped"?** If you have pieces that aren't exerting an influence on the action, make a plan to get them into the game! Don't keep "reserves" in chess! If your overall position is bottled up, giving you little territory, make a plan to free yourself, even if it takes sacrificing a pawn or two. Your King should stay safely at home during the middlegame, of course.

5. **Are there *open* or *semi-open* files for my Rooks or Queen?**

6. **Does my opponent have a weakness that will let me use one of the Dirty Dozen?** Keep the Terrible Twelve Tactics from Chapter 7 in mind–the basic tools for getting things done on the chessboard!

Candidate moves don't run for office, but they do need your vote

Many times when it is your turn to move, you'll be torn between several possible moves. Chess players have developed a terminology and a method to help you deal with this challenge. Each move that suggests itself as a possibly good move is called a *candidate move*. You should make a mental list of your *candidate moves.* Consider each one and its possible outcomes in turn. Do this relatively quickly. Then go back and re-examine the one—or, at most, two—*candidate moves* you favor. Look a bit more deeply. If it remains your favorite, play it!

Some stand-alone computers with a display will show you the *candidate moves* being considered, along with evaluations, while the computer is thinking. Watching your computer analyze a position in a game against you can be very interesting, and can give you some hints about what it thinks the important squares and pieces are.

Pawns: the soul of chess

André Philidor, one of Paris's most famous operatic composers and the world's strongest chess player in the 1700s, said, "Pawns are the soul of chess." He understood that the condition of the pawns can determine a lot about a position, including suggesting a plan of action for the middlegame. In analyzing a middlegame position to decide on a plan, we must always pay attention to the *pawn skeleton*—the pattern of the pawns—on which the muscles and flesh of the game are built.

> **Analyzing the "pawn skeleton" of a chess position can help you to find a good plan. If your opponent has serious pawn weaknesses, your plan could be to prevent him from repairing them and to attack them.**

The chessboard diagram on page 103 shows a host of pawn problems. Let's name and discuss each of them briefly.

Doubled pawns Black's pawns on f7 and f6 are *doubled.* Doubled pawns aren't always bad in the opening or middlegame. But in the

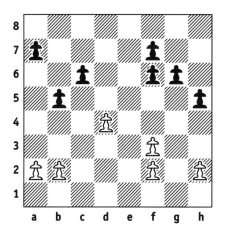

endgame, it's easy to see that they are a serious drawback. After all, they can never defend each other, and the pawn in back is held up by his partner in front. But here's their biggest drawback in the endgame: Even an extra pawn can't produce a *passed pawn* if it's doubled. If your computer gives you a *doubled pawn* in the middlegame, don't panic. When the time is right, try to advance it to trade it off, repairing your pawns.

Isolated pawns White's pawn on d4 is *isolated*. It has no friendly pawns as neighbors. In a popular pseudo-psychological term, it's lost its support system. Isolated center pawns—especially the d-pawn (it's supported by the Queen)—can actually be strong in the opening and middlegame, but as the ending approaches, all isolated pawns "spread gloom over the entire board," as Tartakover said. If you have one, trade it off for a healthy enemy pawn before the ending. If your computer (or any opponent, for that matter) has one, block it with one of your *minor pieces.* Your Knights make especially good blockaders of isolated center pawns. Blockading an isolated pawn is possible *because* it's isolated. Your pieces can't take up residence in front of *connected pawns,* because their neighbors will evict them by threatening capture!

Doubled and isolated pawns These are the terminally ill of the chessboard. White's f-pawns in the diagram above illustrate this ugly weakness. Avoid them as you would pyramid marketing schemes. If you can inflict them on your opponent through even exchanges, do so! They are a serious *positional disadvantage.* If your opponent has them, blockade them to prevent his advancing them to trade them off. Make him live with them until the ending, when your King will emerge to attack them.

Backward pawns aren't unintelligent, just weak Black's c-pawn above is *backward.* Like an *isolated pawn,* it can't be protected by a neighbor. When a *backward* pawn stands on a *half-open* file, as here, it is particularly vulnerable. When your opponent has such a pawn, place one of your Rooks on the file in front of it. Do what's necessary to keep it from advancing and trading itself off for a healthier pawn. And try to make it impossible for your opponent to plant a piece in front of his weak, backward pawn. For example, in the position above, refrain from 1. b2-b4, because you would lose control of c4.

All of the above pawn formations are at least potentially weak. There are other pawn formations that may or may not be weak.

Pawn chains These are diagonally adjacent pawns of the same color. Above, Black has a *pawn chain* from f7 to h5 and from c6 to b5. Pawn chains can be weak or strong, but they are normally double-edged. Whether or not your Bishops are restricted by your own pawn chains is a crucial test of your own pawn chains (see "Good and bad Bishops," below). Usually an enemy pawn chain should be attacked at its base: the pawn in the chain that is nearest your opponent's home rank.

Pawn islands A *pawn island* is a group of connected pawns of the same color. A pawn island ends when there is a file without a friendly pawn. In the diagram on page 103, Black has two pawn islands, and White has four. (His d- and h-pawns are each single-pawn islands.) In general, it is better to have fewer pawn islands.

Queenside majority

Because the center is contested in a well-played chess game, leading to the exchange of center pawns, the *pawn skeletons* are normally divided into two *pawn islands* at an early stage, normally the opening. When one player has more pawns on the queenside than his opponent, he has the *queenside majority*. Since Kings normally castle on the kingside, the *queenside majority* can be an advantage in the *endgame*, because it can produce a *distant passed pawn*. The *queenside majority* is not an automatic advantage by any means, but it can be a threat, especially as the *endgame* looms closer.

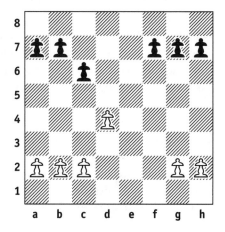

White has the queenside majority.

> Play the middlegame with an eye toward the endgame! And if you can steer your game into one of those highly favorable endings in Chapter 3, do it!

The center in the middlegame

The center is a constant consideration in the middlegame. You'll see that your computer will try to maintain control here. So should you.

- ✓ Maintain center control.
- ✓ Don't attack unless you control the center.
- ✓ If you are attacked on the wing, counter in the center!
- ✓ Keep your Knights near the center, so they can jump to action on either side.

The strategic importance of the center can determine the choices you make with your pawns. When you have a choice of pawns to recapture with, it is generally best to capture *toward the center.*

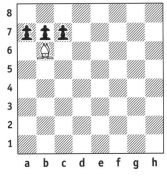

Black has a choice of pawns to capture the Bishop. As a general principle, he should capture toward the center.

Count your change!

The center is so important that it affects the value of the pawns by their location. As pawns get farther and farther away from the center, they are worth less and less. One way to remember this is, in the opening and middlegame, a center pawn (e- and d-pawns) is worth $1. Pawns on the f-file are worth 90 cents, g-pawns are worth 80 cents, and Rook pawns are worth 70 cents. But be careful, these values can turn around in the endgame, when an *outside passed pawn* is the King of peons.

Good and bad Bishops

Bishops and Rooks are especially influenced by the *pawn skeleton*. Rooks, as we've seen, should generally be placed on *open* and *half-open files* in the middlegame. Because of their great power, they can stay on the home rank and still exert influence. Bishops require more care. Because they travel only on the diagonals, they can be restricted—cramped—by pawn chains on their own color. Look at this example. ▶

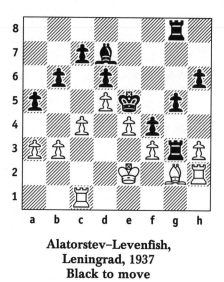

**Alatorstev–Levenfish,
Leningrad, 1937
Black to move**

You can see that White's light-square Bishop is hemmed in badly by his own pawns. The White player has been tempted to place nearly all his pawns on the same color squares as his remaining Bishop. The two *pawn chains,* b3-d5 and f3-d5, leave the Bishop almost no moves. White's Bishop is an extreme case—it's a very *bad Bishop.* The bad Bishop is really a special case of the *cramped position*—something always to be avoided.

Black's light-square Bishop is a *good Bishop.* The Black pawn chains are on the its opposite color, not in any way affecting the Bishop's mobility. As a matter of fact, they complement the Bishop, because these pawns control squares the Bishop can't. They're a perfect team with the Bishop. Black won by advancing his g-pawn. White's pieces were just too congested to put up a successful defense.

Opposite-color Bishops

We saw in Chapter 3 that when you and your opponent have Bishops that travel on different-colored squares in the *end-game,* the chances of a draw are tremendously increased, because the Bishops can never make contact. However, in the middle-game, with many other pieces on the board, *opposite-color Bishops* are a great help to the attacker, since the defender is effectively a piece down on one of the colors of the board. The position at right shows this idea in action.

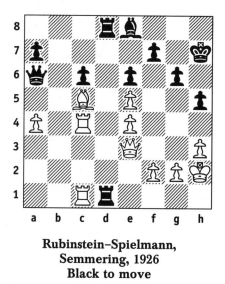

**Rubinstein–Spielmann,
Semmering, 1926
Black to move**

In the opening, Black *fianchettoed* his Bishop on g7, in front of his castled King. This is a popular plan today. Your computer will certainly adopt it occasionally. The idea is to have great influence on the a1-h8 diagonal throughout the game. But here, Black has been forced to trade it off, leaving him unprotected on the dark squares around his King. His remaining Bishop can't travel on those square, and, besides, it's a very much a *bad Bishop*.

Black played 1. ... Rd1xc1? here, assuming that White would have to recapture with the Rook on c4, trading down some power—a good thing to do when under attack. Here, however, White has one of the Dirty Dozen at his disposal: a winning *in-between move* that ignores the Black Rook for a more important goal! He played 2. Bc5-f8! Now, whatever Black does, even including a sacrificial check on h1 with his extra Rook, White will checkmate him with his Queen and Bishop. White's 2. Bc5-f8! seems like magic, but he found it by applying logic. Black's kingside dark squares are unguarded by pieces or pawns, and his pieces have lost contact with his King! By the way, the computers had an easy time finding 2. Bc5-f8.

Knights vs. Bishops in the middlegame

Bishops are swashbucklers—at their best in wide-open games with many clear files and diagonals. In such positions, their long-range abilities come to the fore, as a Bishop can zoom across the board in a single move. In such positions, don't let your computer trade one of its Knights for one of your effective Bishops!

The Knights excel in positions that make the Bishops uncomfortable. When the position is *closed*, without open files and diagonals, the Knight is in its glory because it is the only piece that can jump over these obstacles. If you have such a position against your computer, or any other opponent, don't trade your Knights for Bishops!

Your Knight's mobility is drastically reduced when you put it on the edge of the board. Put one there and count the squares it can leap to. Then put it in the center and count its moves. You'll be convinced! As the great Dr. Siegbert Tarrasch put it: "A Knight on the rim is dim!" Or as Tartakover said, "Some Knights don't leap, they limp!" Make sure yours are in the bright sunshine and leaping. Keep them *near* the center!

> **Bishop and Knight begin as equal in value, but their relative value depends on the position, chiefly on the *pawn skeleton*. *Wide-open* positions favor the Bishop; *closed*, the Knight.**

Rooks and Queens in the middlegame

We've often said that Rooks—both in the opening and the middlegame—belong on *open* or *half-open* files. Queens often do their best on such files as well, but not always, since they have the option of operating powerfully on diagonals. So you have a choice with your Queen, depending on where you want to apply pressure to your opponent.

But Rooks are straight-ahead and sideways warriors only. In the middlegame on an open file, they flex their muscles.

The ultimate goal of a Rook or Queen on the open or semi-open file is to *penetrate* the opponent's home ranks. A Rook safely on the enemy's seventh—or, in White's camp, the second—rank puts tremendous pressure on the opponent's camp. And doubled Rooks there can create a collapse!

Pawn storm your plastic partner!

As a matter of fact, the topic of invading ranks brings up an important middlegame suggestion for play against your computer. Your computer will almost always castle kingside. When you can reasonably castle to the other side of the board, try it—especially when your computer has *fianchettoed* his Bishop on g7. This leaves you with a ready-made plan that is long-term and well beyond the horizon of your computer: the *pawn storm against the King*. It can be deadly.

Castling on the opposite side from your computer's King prepares you to launch a *pawn storm*, an attack that can take advantage of the *horizon effect*.

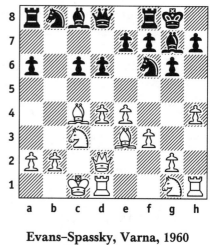

Evans–Spassky, Varna, 1960
White to move

Playing against Larry Evans, the great American player and one of the greatest chess writers of all time, Boris Spassky, a future World Champion, plans the *pawn storm*. Shifting his King to the queenside, he advances his kingside pawns to open lines against the Black King. The fact that Black has *fianchettoed* makes this plan stronger, because the pawn on g6 becomes an early, and inflexible, contact point between the storming pawns and the defensive ones.

To confirm how straightforward, easy-to-play, and crushing the pawn storm can be, co-author Al Lawrence took on the powerful ChessMaster 5000, set at its Expert level running on our same 200 Pentium configuration used in all tests of the software programs. Using set-up mode, he started the game at the above position, and made all of his moves very quickly, relying on general principles.

Lawrence vs. ChessMaster 5000

1. ...   Qd8-c7
A better try here was countering in the center with 1. ... d5, as Evans played against Spassky in the original game, or, perhaps even better, slowing the White pawn storm with 1. ... h5.

2. h4-h5!
A move instantly made by a human! Al admitted to having only one *candidate move*, so he played it! The whole point of White's set-up is to advance his kingside pawns before Black can organize a defense.

2.	...	Nf6xh5
3.	g2-g4	Nh5-f6
4.	Be3-h6	Bg7xh6
5.	Qd2xh6	▶

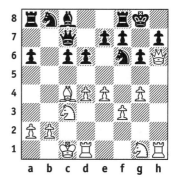

Black is in a hopeless position after only a few easy-to-find moves by White. White's artillery is breathing down the Black King's neck on the half-open h-file.

For the record, the rest of the game, including a well-known sacrifice of Rook for Knight on h5 to break apart Black's defenses, went: 5. ... Nbd8-d7 6. g4-g5 Nf6-h5 7. Rh1xh5 g6xh5 8. Qh6xh5 e7-e6 9. Ng1-e2 Rf8-e8 10. Rd1-h1 Nd7-f8 11. e4-e5 d6-d5 12. Bc4-d3 Bc8-b7 13. Bd3xh7+ Nf8xh7 14. Qh5xh7+ Kg8-f8 15. g5-g6 Kf8-e7 16. Qh7xf7+ Ke7-d8 17. Qf7-f6+ Kd8-c8 18. Rh1-h7 Qc7-d8 19. Qf6-f7 Ra8-a7 20. Ne2-f4 Kc8-b8 21. Nf4xe6, and it's hopeless for Black.

White's kingside *pawn storm* led to a rout of ChessMaster 5000 because the coming impact of the advancing kingside pawns was beyond the computer program's horizon.

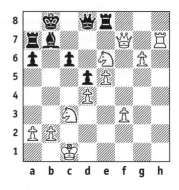

Lawrence–ChessMaster 5000
After White's 21. Nf4xe6

Wherever your middlegame exploits take you, remember what separates you from the computer that fits into the palm of your hand: planning and the ability to apply general principles!

Remember! When most of the pieces are traded off, you've come to the endgame! Change gears to the principles you studied in Chapter 3!

Cramped positions bear the germs of their own defeat.
–Grandmaster Siegbert Tarrasch, M.D.

It was your fault, Garry.
—Film tough-guy Charles Bronson to
World Champion Garry Kasparov in an
elevator in the Plaza Hotel, New York,
after the 1997 Deep Blue match

CHAPTER NINE

Chess as Silent Movie, or Oh, No! He's Tied Himself to the Railroad Tracks!*

Garry Kasparov, brooding, dark, and handsome hero of the silent screen. Hands tensely cover his face except for his burning eyes. He shakes his head, framed by closely cut dark curls, from side-to-side in an agony of effort to come to the rescue. Pushing his Queen to temporary safety, he jumps up to pace the room. He's frantic, but always voiceless—obviously desperate over whether he will be able to foil the next dastardly move. The conflict is clear. All that's missing is the piano music.

People all over the world are riveted to this all too brief slice of chess life. The silent melodrama unfolds wherever they are. On-site viewers see it on the giant monitors inside the Equitable skyscraper's packed and ironically subterranean auditorium—or up on the building's 50th floor with its panoramic views of midtown Manhattan where the press room bustles with dozens of the world's best-known journalists standing behind hand-held microphones or sitting in front of laptops linked to their newspapers and magazines. At home, we simply turn on CNN, our global-village newspaper. During the last game of the match, I spoke with a TV-watching friend in France, who, in the middle of a sentence, actually exclaimed, "*Mon Dieu*! Man lost!"

*Based on an article by Al Lawrence in the July 1997 issue of *Chess Life*, published by the U.S. Chess Federation, reprinted here with permission. Copyright by Al Lawrence.

Only, the villain of this silent movie doesn't have a black mustache to twist. In fact, it doesn't have a body at all, unless you want to count two side-by-side monolithic towers like the one timidly but compulsively touched by the evolving apes in Kubrick's *2001*, long after movies had turned to talkies. But if the rules of the game called for IBM's Deeper Blue to throw a young widow out into the snow for being unable to raise the back rent, rest assured it would do so without a trace of remorse, or of any other emotion.

Deeper Blue isn't really even physically present. Like a sci-fi body snatcher, it adds insult to ego-injury by using humans—several of its programmers—to sit across from the World Champion and make moves they see displayed on a computer monitor, moves they don't understand. For by their own admission, these interchangeable limbs of the supercomputer they've filled with masterly moves are chess tyros. In the match last year, one even became confused and made the incorrect move, not the one Deep Blue had dictated.

These front men for the computer amount to bizzaro versions of the late 19th-century automaton called Mephisto, the chess-playing "machine" constructed by Londoner Charles Godfrey Gumpel, a manu-

facturer of artificial limbs. To the amazed spectators of its day, Mephisto appeared mechanical from the outside. But on the *inside* hid the diminutive and flexible human master, Isidor Gunsberg.

It's not just a pretty Mary Pickford, fear exquisitely delineated on her girl-next-door face, whom Garry tried to save; it's us. And not just those of us who play chess, but all of us who would like to keep believing, for just a little while longer, that there's something special, poetic, and uniquely effective about the way humans—or at least the most creative of us—think. IBM tries to downplay this angle. After all, they don't want us to be threatened by their computers. But what else is going on here? What else explains the world's fascination? Okay, chess will go on despite Garry's valiant but failed rescue effort. Most of us will not be too bothered by the fact that a human chess player can no longer lay undisputed claim to playing better than machines. But we'll not fully forget the closing scene.

Our collective pulses jack-hammering in our ears, the music reaches a crescendo. We see Garry, tied by his own hands, with theatrically copious coils of rope, to the railroad tracks. The locomotive steaming down on him, he seems to realize too late that since the hero is himself in the trap, there's no one to come to the rescue. In the end, Garry is dazed and doomed. His eyes, now with dark circles under them, plaintively accuse the producers of rewriting the script at the last minute–did they allow Deeper Blue's handlers to inject new info during a game? Garry falls victim to a cynical, post-modern twist on the old silent movie plots: The villain wins. The curtain crashes down just before we'd have to see blood; lights come up. And the 1997 audience doesn't even hiss, but merely whimpers a resigned, "Well, sooner or later it had to happen."

Unlike fellow defender-of-humans-against-their-creations John Henry, Garry couldn't keep up with the new machine that does his job. But also unlike the legendary steel-driving man, Garry, in real life, lives to make another movie. Next time he's holding out for rights to script approval.

You won't get another rematch from them.
–Charles Bronson, stepping
off the elevator.

*There's not the mystery in ten murders
that there is in one game of chess.*
–Sir Arthur Conan Doyle

CHAPTER TEN

Putting It All Together—
Human Beats ChessMaster

A chess game–even with its three stages of opening, middlegame, and endgame–is an organic whole. Plenty of players have "won" the opening only to lose to superior endgame play, or even to fall victim to checkmate in a furious middlegame attack. In this chapter you'll see how a tournament "B" player coordinated all three phases to conquer a very strong software program, ChessMaster 4000.

Bob Irons (USCF-rated 1721) vs. ChessMaster 4000

1. d2-d4   Ng8-f6
Black prevents White from playing 2. e2-e4, setting up the broad pawn center. Black's Knight hits d5 as well.

2. c2-c4   e7-e6
Challenges the control of d5. So White's c-pawn and Black's e-pawn are warring over the same square, even though they are not standing adjacent to one another.

3. Nb1-c3
White again threatens to play e4 and get a dominating center, since this move protects e4.

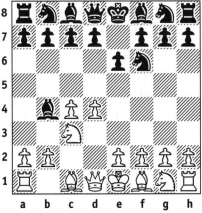

3. ...   Bf8-b4 ▶
Black *pins* White's newly developed Knight. Without actually capturing it, he counteracts its influence on e4, and therefore he

once again prevents White from advancing his e-pawn two squares.

This opening pattern, like most of them, has a name. It's called the Nimzo-Indian Defense, in recognition of the work of Grandmaster Aaron Nimzovitch (1886–1935). Certainly, these moves had been played before, but without a great understanding of their significance. During the 1920s, Nimzovitch forged the underlying ideas into a complete strategic system against 1. d4.

Nimzovitch was a "hypermodernist." He and his followers held that, to control the center, one didn't have to occupy it. You can see this idea at work here. Black doesn't own a pawn in the center box of squares e4/d4/e5/d5, but nevertheless he's fighting for control of this highground. Nimzovitch had many literary feuds with another of our favorite players, Dr. Siegbert Tarrasch. From the previous generation of "Classicists," Tarrasch believed strongly that the center should be occupied. In a sense, the argument still goes on many years later, reflected in this game between a man and his computer! But Nimzovitch's ideas are now universally accepted as being as valid as Dr. Tarrasch's.

> *The man with a new idea is a Crank,*
> *until the idea succeeds.*
> —Mark Twain

Nimzovitch was one of the game's genuine characters, by the way. He used to stand on his head in the corner of the crowded tournament room before a game, to get the blood to his brain. And once, losing a tournament game to a much less accomplished master, he jumped on the table—amid all the other participants and spectators—and screamed, "Why must I lose to this idiot?" What would he have said if he had lived long enough to lose an occasional game to our computer friends?

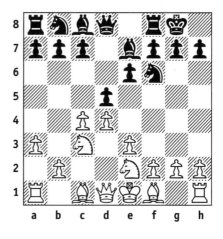

4.	e2-e3	0-0
5.	Ng1-e2	d7-d5
6.	a2-a3	Bb4-e7 ▶

Black's Bishop was attacked by 6. a2-a3 and he doesn't want to trade Bishop for Knight without gaining something. Here, capturing the

Knight on c3 with the Bishop wouldn't result in doubled c-pawns for White, because White simply recaptures with his other Knight. So Black does the right thing and retreats the Bishop to a good square, where it can't be further harassed, and from where it can control many squares. And retreating it won't turn out to be a waste of time if White can't make something useful out of his a3.

7. c4xd5   e6xd5

Black has developed his kingside pieces, castled, and has his share of the center. White's position seems a little congested already. For example, his Knight on e2 blocks his Bishop on f1, which in turn, keeps him from castling into safety. But White has a longer-term plan in mind, one that involves building up a kingside attack. We've seen that such a long-term middlegame plan offers threats beyond the horizon of chess computer's number-crunching. It would be interesting to know the computer's evaluation of the position. Let's see how this plan unfolds.

8. b2-b4   a7-a5
9. b4-b5

White, having played a2-a3, makes a queenside demonstration, gaining a little space. Black correctly challenges this wing operation with a7-a5, contesting the space and separating White's a- and b- pawns to weaken their influence.

9. ...   Nb8-d7 ▶

After some good moves, Black begins to become a little too passive for the sharp position to come. Here we would prefer c7-c5, rechallenging both the center and the queenside, since the pawn attacks both d4 and b4. One has to assume that White has followed one of our basic rules of playing computers—he seems to have gotten the computer out of its "opening book"

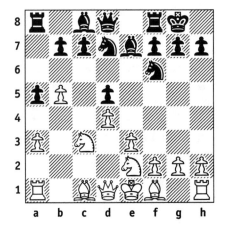

early. The computer must think on its own, sometimes revealing the effects of the *horizon effect* and the program's limited knowledge of opening principles.

10.	Ne2-g3	Nd7-b6
11.	Bf1-d3	Be7-d6 ▶

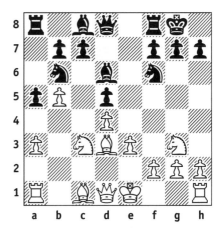

Compare the logic of White's last two moves with that of Black's. White has a long-range plan to attack Black's castled King. His last two moves clearly bear down on that area of the board, while significantly uncramping his own position. Black's last moves aren't so good. The Knight on b6 is too far away from Black's King to offer protection. Remember, the Knight is a short-range piece; to defend the King, it must be close. The Black Bishop on d6 has now been moved three times in the opening–surely not a good idea, since its latest home is certainly no big improvement.

12.	0-0	Bd6xg3
13.	h2xg3	a5-a4? ▶

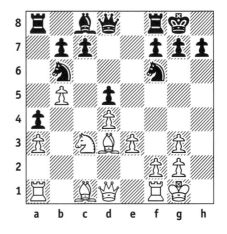

Again, compare this snapshot with the previous diagram. White gets more and more chances to build his attack in the center and eventually on the kingside. He's now castled into safety, while Black has moved his Bishop *four* times, trading it off for a Knight, probably to reduce White's influence on e4. The computer's 13. ... a5-a4? artificially *isolates* White's b-pawn by separating it from its a-pawn partner, but this is a great example of the computer applying principles not suitable for this moment in the opening. Its idea is too slow. It should start coordinating its kingside defenses for the upcoming siege. But, once again, like Scarlett O'Hara, it can't think about that today. The *horizon effect*!

When your house is on fire, you can't be bothered with the neighbors. Or, as we say in chess, if your King is under attack, you don't worry about losing a pawn on the queenside.
–World Champion Garry Kasparov

14. f2-f3	Bc8-e6
15. Nc3-e2	Qd8-d7
16. e3-e4	d5xe4
17. f3xe4	Be6-b3
18. Qd1-d2	Rf8-e8 ▶

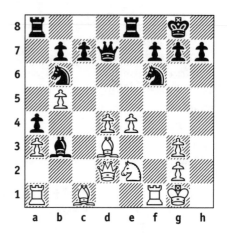

Let's now take a long and careful look at this position.

White has used a famous idea of former World Champion Mikhail Botvinnik: a pawn at f3 to support an e4 thrust. His 15. Nc3-e2 showed that he was a human with a plan. He wants to have his short-range Knight on the kingside, where he will soon have overwhelming superiority. And he wanted to bolster his pawn on d4 so that he could advance its previous defender on e3. When Black exchanges on e4, White has an unchallenged, mobile pawn center, as well as a *half-open* f-file–a pathway for heavy artillery shells to hit the Black fortress. Nicely done!

Meanwhile, the computer is again showing its lack of orientation. It moves its remaining Bishop a *second time* with 17. Be6-b3, forcing White to move his Queen to a better square. Black's 18. ... Rf8-e8, following the principle of grabbing the semi-open file, is out of place here because Black has the higher imperative of defending his King! So the computer has illogically chosen the wrong principle. Black should be trying to exchange off the attacking pieces. Logic would recommend 18. ... Bb3-c4, trying to rid the board of White's threatening light-square Bishop.

We're now in a middlegame showing the deficiencies in the computer's opening play. Black has no center and badly placed pieces. White has reached a moment that reminds us again of Wilhelm Steinitz's dictum that, achieving superiority, we must strike or forever lose the opportunity.

We go on:

19. Rf1xf6!   g7xf6

White gives up the *Exchange* at exactly the right moment to *eliminate the defender*–the only one faithfully standing by his monarch! At the same time, he doubles and isolates Black's f-pawns, shredding the King's cover.

20. e4-e5   Bb3-c4   ▶

The computer wants too late to try to trade off the threatening White pieces. If it had tried 20. ... f6-f5, White would win the pawn after 21. Qd2-g5+ and then 22. Bd3xf5, attacking the Black Queen while breathing down the neck of the Black King. Take a minute before reading on. Look for another flashy move White could make in the diagram at right. Of course, it's against the Black King.

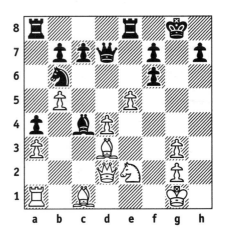

◀

21. Bd3xh7+!   Kg8-h8

If instead, the computer captures the Bishop with 21. ... Kg8xh7, White forces mate! The computer sees now—too late!—what it could not see over its *horizon* when it played 20. ... Bb3-c4. Let's look ahead at the mating pattern that White threatens down the road. ▼

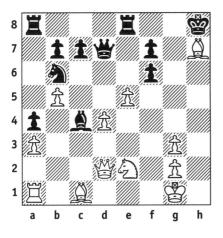

If Black plays 21. ... Kg8xh7, we would have this position. ▼

White would *force* this line: 22. Qd2-h6+ (the Queen is supported by its remaining Bishop) 22. ... Kh7-g8 23. e5xf6 Qd7-g4 (to prevent mate on g7).

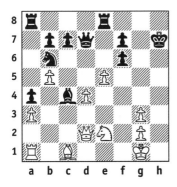

We would then have this position. ▶

The White Knight on e2 has been immune from capture, because White's Queen has been threatening the mating pattern seen above. But now Black's Queen guards g7. This is the position the computer probably relied on when it played 20. ... Bb3-c4. But, because of the *horizon effect*, it did not see the winning move at White's disposal here. Can you see it?

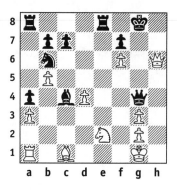

24. Bc1-g5! This blocks the Black Queen from its defense of the g7 square, and mate is unavoidable.

So much for analyzing the "what if" possibility of 21. ... Kg8xh7. We've seen it leads to a *forced mate* against Black! We're back to the diagram on page 119, after Black's 21. ... Kg8-h8.

22. Qd2-h6

Now White has set up a devastating *discovered check*. The fact that he doesn't really have to use it proves the wisdom of Savielly Tartakover, that wag of chess, who said, "The threat is stronger than the execution." ▶

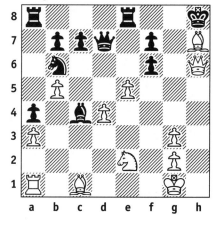

22. ...   Re8xe5

Here, a human player with compassion for himself would resign. But we know all about the ostrich-head-in-sand approach that computers display in this kind of circumstance. As long as mate can be put over their horizons, they can't think about it yet!

23. d4xe5   Qd7-d1+

One more delay of the inevitable!

24. Kg1-h2   Qd1xc1

And again. Giving up its Rook, and then its Queen, because it can't bear to see the final mating picture.

25. Ra1xc1   Nb6-d7

26. e5xf6	Nd7xf6
27. Qh6xf6+	Kh8xh7
28. Rc1xc4	Kh8-g8

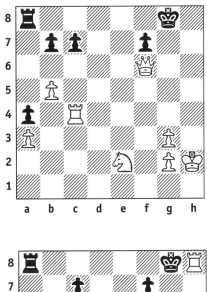

Black has avoided the threatened mating pattern and the discovered check, but he's a cool Queen plus a Knight down without any compensation.

The end is human's play!

29. Rc4-h4	b7-b6

Nothing better to do!

30. Rh4-h8 checkmate

A common mating pattern, worth remembering.

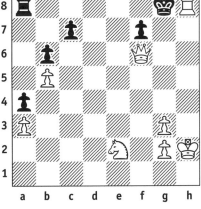

So, the computer never got to dispute endgames with its human opponent because it couldn't find the right defensive plan to stave off White's long-range middlegame attack plan. Actually, the computer just didn't see it in time. As we've shown, such slow build-ups for an attack often work well against computers because of the *horizon effect*. By the time the computer "sees" the attack coming...it's already too late!

Chess above all other games lends itself to the postmortem.
—London *Times*, 1937

The meanings of words are NOT in the words; they are in us.
—S.I. Hayakawa, *Language in Action* (1939)

CHAPTER ELEVEN

Talkin' the Talk—In the Jargon Are the Ideas

The language of chess is unique and packed with images. Chess players love to "talk the talk." An isolated pawn isn't just bad—"It spreads gloom over the entire board." When you're at lunch with chess players, and someone nearly spills his water, he'll grab it quickly and say "*J'adoube*," the ultra-correct, Frenchified chess term making it possible to touch your piece to adjust it on a square without being forced to move it. And if at the same table you complain about your appetizer being eaten by one of your table mates, he's likely to respond, "It was *en prise*, so I captured it."

Knowing the terms does indeed help you remember the ideas. This section will give you some of the basic vocabulary of chess and computer chess. As you look at the listings, you'll see that you've picked up quite a bit already. Jargon allows quick, thorough communication in a very short exchange. In fact, it can allow communication to be too intense. Take an incident involving an offhand game between co-author Al Lawrence and his friend Fairfield W. Hoban, Esq., one day in Washington Square Park. Al enjoys telling this in his own words:

Fairfield was a major-league New York City Character with a capital "C." He looked to be a wonderfully distinguished man in his 60s, with his handsome, gray mustache, schnauzer-like goatee, and his impeccable dress. In fact, he had many distinguished accomplishments: Columbia University, Harvard Law, Director of the Peace Corps in Pakistan in the Camelot years of the early 1960s, advisor to emerging democracies. But deep inside beat the heart of a cunning, nine-year-old brat, ever threatening to emerge.

Fairfield loved chess. He knew more about its history and its anecdotes than anyone I've ever met. And he knew his Philidor. He had chosen his seat in front of the concrete chess table so that the afternoon sun shone directly in my eyes. And we had stopped at a Greenwich Village Indian restaurant for lunch, which somehow had included brown bottles of Taj Mahal beer for me, but cardamom tea for him.

The game went on in a familiar pattern. Fairfield got a miserable game in the opening, hung on by his fingernails in the early middlegame, and set diabolical traps in the late middlegame. To this day, I believe he arranged this sequence on purpose. Nothing filled him with glee like a comeback.

Throughout this phase of the game, Fairfield riveted his attention to the board. But he would make comments intended to distract me, without losing his own concentration.

"Queen *en prise*," Fairfield said, his unmoving, almost unblinking stare remaining with pinpoint focus on the chess armies he'd managed to tangle into a dizzying confusion in order to trick his way out of a losing position.

Did he mean the lovely and solitaire young woman walking by? Fairfield's head never moved. Perhaps mine had *accidentally* turned slightly toward the woman.

Remembering that it was my move, I began again to concentrate, just when a policeman on horseback clip-clopped by for the third or fourth time.

"Knight's tour," said Fairfield.

Just silly enough to distract me, I realized. How did I let him drag me into these complications, I thought to myself. He always does this. Will I ever learn?

"Doubled pawns," Fairfield said. My eye caught a young mother walking past, pushing one of those twin baby carriages, identical babies dozing in the autumn sunshine in pink frills and complete trust.

I winced, but couldn't help looking. The sun bothered me. My head seemed just the faintest bit light. Suddenly, without my control, my hand shot out to the board and made a hasty move that my brain had just begun to consider. Uh-oh, I thought, arching over the board to see the consequences of what I'd done. What have I gotten into now? A school teacher leading her primary school class on a field trip came by on the sidewalk right next to us, all the kids in tow, holding hands in a long line.

"Pawn chain," Fairfield said.

He was getting to me, even after all these years. I was becoming confused about what was on the board and what was off. Relax, I thought, coincidence will stop feeding him these punch lines. I'm a believer in the odds, you see. The position on the board was critical. It still looked to me that I would win, if I was just careful and didn't allow him to pull off one of his tricks. But where were these mistakes hiding? Ah, I began to see his ploy.

At that moment, the lovely Sunday afternoon delivered to Fairfield a gift he would always recall with what the greatest of German chess writers, Siegbert Tarrasch, would have called *Schadenfreude*: the joy of the misery of others, in this case mine. Two men in religious frock—white collars, black jackets and pants, one Caucasian, one Afro-American—walked leisurely toward us down the long sidewalk that runs through the center of the park, linking one corner to another. I was now too much a part of this off-the-board game, and vaguely knew what was coming. But like a punch in the nose, seeing it coming only made it sting worse.

"Bishops of opposite color—on the same long diagonal!" Master of the stone face, even Fairfield couldn't forestall just a tweak of a smile at his good fortune.

My reply was yet another distracted move, and then I saw, too late, Fairfield's trap. For a moment, I became annoyed with the very things I loved—annoyed with Fair, annoyed with the sun, with the lingering effects of the lunch, and most of all, annoyed with the teeming activity in the park. I felt a bit like Meursault, Camus' pitiable protagonist, who became a stranger to his own life because of a few awkward physical distractions. Why hadn't I gone to lunch with my beautiful wife, Daphne? She's *nice* to me! Fairfield had found his save. He could slide his Queen back and forth, checking me forever into a draw, like the one in the example in Chapter 3. I couldn't escape the perpetual.

Then all at once I realized the obvious—the park wasn't giving Fairfield any special help. The world was there, and so was chess, in all their diversities. There simply wasn't anything or anyone passing by whom Fairfield couldn't turn to his advantage.

I perked up, felt the challenge, again heard the birds' song. I looked hastily about for my own weapon. After all, life's panoply was just as willing to be on my side. Of course!

Of the literally thousands of dog-walkers to come by the park that day, the perfect one was close enough—and the feisty schnauzer even looked young. I looked at Fair, I looked at the schnauzer. Perhaps there was an outside intelligence at work here after all.

Fair caught sight of my little, furry gray ally just a split-second too late to take the initiative, and tweaked his own mustache— a gesture of surprised self-recognition.

"Pup,"* I said.

Perceptive sport that he was, Fairfield stuck out his hand in the time-honored gesture we used after every game, despite our long familiarity. His slate-blue eyes under John L. Lewis eyebrows, previously narrowed in struggle, opened to a twinkle. "Yes, it's a draw," he said. "But I thought I had you there for a moment."

*Chess jargon for perpetual check, when one side keeps checking the other without respite—a draw.

Fairfield W. Hoban, Esq., the man who could turn jargon into a weapon

Glossary of Terms

Action chess: Chess played at a time control of thirty minutes per game per person.

Algebraic notation: A method of recording moves in which each square is named for its intersecting rank (1 through 8) and file (a through h). Nd4 means that the Knight (N) has just moved to the fourth rank of the Queen (d) file.

Back-rank mate: A checkmate delivered by a Queen or Rook, in which the enemy King is trapped on the back (first or eighth) rank, usually by his own men.

Backward pawn: A pawn whose neighboring pawns have been pushed forward. Backward pawns may be weak due to lack of protection by other pawns.

Bishop: A minor piece, about equal in value to a Knight. Bishops move diagonally (any direction) and therefore have access only to squares of one color.

Bishops of opposite colors: A situation where each opponent has a Bishop, one controlling the light squares and the other controlling the dark squares.

Blitz chess: Chess played at a very fast time control—normally five minutes per player per game (a.k.a. speed chess).

Blunder: A very unfortunate move.

Book: Within known opening theory. A move can be "book" or "out of book"–not part of theory.

Bughouse: A form of *blitz* chess played by four players (two per team) with two sets. Each captured piece is passed to the adjacent board, where that player may place it anywhere on the board, and this counts as his/her move. The first player to win wins for his/her team.

Building a bridge: An endgame technique in which a Rook creates shelter for a King and/or a pawn (see also Lucena position).

Caissa: The mythological goddess of chess.

Candidate moves: The set of moves under consideration at any given time during a game.

Castling: A move in which the King travels two squares from its original position to either side, then the Rook on that side comes around the King and stands next to it. Written as 0-0 or 0-0-0 (depending on which side) in all types of chess notation.

Center: The four squares in the middle of the board, namely d4, d5, e4 and e5. Fighting for control of the center is a critical opening strategy.

Check: A condition in which the King is under direct attack.

Checkmate: A condition in which the King is checked and cannot get out of check. That's all, folks!

Closed file: A file occupied by pawns of both colors.

Closed game: The type of game that naturally develops from pawns being blocked in the center. Usually arises from the moves 1. d2-d4 d7-d5.

Combination: A series of forcing moves resulting in any improved position.

Consolidation: The process of coordinating and/or trading pieces in order to stabilize one's position.

Dead position: A position with no tactics.

Decoy: A chess piece (or a pawn) used to distract the opponent from more immediate positional concerns.

Deflection: Coaxing a defending piece away from its post.

Descriptive notation: An old-fashioned way of recording the moves. Files are designated not by letters, but by the names of the pieces that occupy those files in the original starting position. Rank names are dependent on whose point of view it is. P-QR4 says that a pawn has landed on the fourth rank of the Queen Rook file.

Desperado: *See* Kamikaze.

Development: The moving of pieces from their original squares to more useful squares.

Diagonal: A slanted row of squares running either from corner to corner or from one side of the board to the adjacent side.

Discovered check: A check on the enemy King via *discovery*.

Discovery: The act of attacking with a piece by moving another piece out of its way.

Double attack: An attack on two pieces at once.

Double check: A condition in which two pieces are checking the King at once (by way of *discovery*).

Doubled pawns: Two friendly pawns occupying the same file. Doubled pawns are often weak, since they cannot protect each other.

Doubled rooks: Two friendly Rooks occupying the same rank or file.

Draw: A tied game.

Draw by perpetual check: A draw resulting when one player checks another *ad infinitum.*

Draw by repetition: A draw resulting from repeating the same position three (not necessarily consecutive) times.

Dubious move: A move that is intuitively considered doubtful, but is not proven to be bad.

Elo system: The currently used system of rating chess, named for its developer, Arpad Elo (1903–1990), an American statistician born in Hungary.

Endgame: The last of the three phases of a chess game, in which most, if not all, pieces have been traded off.

En passant: A quirky rule of chess by which a pawn on its own fifth rank may capture an adjacent pawn by landing on the square directly behind this pawn. This can only be done immediately following the captured pawn's first move.

En prise: A term used for a piece that is completely unprotected, and therefore available for immediate capture. Such a piece is also said to be "hanging."

Exchange (the): Difference in value between a Rook and a *minor piece.*

Exclam: A slang term used by chess players to indicate a very good move– written as a exclamation point in all chess notation.

Fianchetto: An Italian word used to denote the Bishop's development toward the side (flank) of the board instead of toward the center. This allows the Bishop to occupy the longest possible diagonal.

FIDE: Fédération Internationale des Échecs, a.k.a. the World Chess Feder-ation.

File: Any of the eight vertical rows of squares, lettered *a* through *h* in algebraic notation.

Fish: Slang for a very weak player, particularly one who plays for money.

Fixed pawns: Two enemy pawns blocking each other's way so that neither one can move.

Flank opening: An opening featuring a *fianchettoed* Bishop.

Flight square: Any square to which a piece can safely flee (a.k.a. escape square).

Fool's mate: The shortest game ending in mate (two moves). For example, 1. g4, e5; 2. f3, Qh4 mate.

Forfeit: The loss of a game due either to overstepping the time limit or a penalty imposed by the tournament director.

Fork: An attack on two or more enemy pieces with a single piece.

Gambit: A material sacrifice (usually a pawn) in exchange for some kind of advantage.

Half-open file: A file occupied by pawns of one color only.

Hanging: *See En prise.*

Horizon effect: A weakness in the play of chess computers, caused by an inflexibility in their search methods. When facing inevitable material loss, a computer might unnecessarily weaken its position or sacrifice lesser material to push the loss beyond its "search horizon" (the number of moves ahead that a computer is able to see).

Human: The world's strongest chess computer.

Initiative: The ability to call the shots. (The attacking player has the initiative.)

Isolated pawn: A pawn with no other pawns on the files adjacent to it. These tend to be weak since they cannot be protected by other pawns.

***J'adoube*:** Literally, "I adjust." A French term uttered by a player desiring to center a piece on a square, without having to move the piece (see Touch-move).

Kamikaze: The act of a trapped and threatened (unsavable) piece sacrificing itself for the most that it can get. A Knight which is hopelessly lost, for example, might as well capture a pawn if possible (a.k.a. "desperado").

Kibitzer: A pesky individual who comments on games in progress, offering players a wealth of unsolicited and often useless advice.

King: The most valued of the chess pieces. The head honcho. A King moves one square in any direction.

Kingside: The side of the board with the Kings, in their original positions, on it.

Knight: A minor piece, about equal in value to a Bishop.

Knight's tour: A puzzle whose object is to move a Knight to every square on an empty board, visiting each square only once.

LCD: Liquid Crystal Display; that which enables you to see information on your computer via the screen.

Lucena position: An endgame theme employed to protect a King from Rook checks, using a technique that is called "*building a bridge.*"

***Luft*:** German for "air." *Luft* signifies the creation of a future *flight square* for the King, in order to avoid a *back-rank mate.*

Major piece: A Queen or Rook.

Middlegame: The second of the three phases of a chess game, the point at which development has been completed, but few captures have taken place.

Minor piece: A Knight or a Bishop.

N: Symbol representing a Knight in both algebraic and descriptive notation (K is for King).

Open file: A file with no pawns on it. This is where you want your Rooks!

Open game: A game in which at least one pair of center pawns has been traded.

Opening: The first of the three phases of a chess game. Basic opening strategy consists of *development*, control of the *center*, and *castling* into safety.

Opposition: An endgame-related theme, where Kings *oppose* each other, in which the player who doesn't have to move holds the upper hand.

OTB: Over the board (generally used as the opposite of *postal chess*).

Overload: The state of a piece having too many functions at once.

Overprotection: The protection of a piece by more pieces than are necessary.

Parting with the Lady: Slang for sacrificing the Queen.

Passed pawn: A pawn with no opposing pawns on the files adjacent to it, which enables it to advance unmolested by enemy pawns.

Patzer: Slang for a very weak player (similar to *fish*).

Pawn: The least valued of all chess pieces (but never underestimate its worth). A pawn moves only forward and captures diagonally.

Pawn chain: Diagonally adjacent pawns of the same color.

Pawn grabber: A chess player who snatches material with dangerous disregard for the consequences.

Pawn promotion: The metamorphosis of a pawn into another piece (usually a Queen) upon reaching the eighth rank.

Pawn skeleton: The configuration and condition of the pawns.

Pawn storm: An attack on the enemy position by several connected pawns.

Pawn structure: Refers to the placement of pawns in any given position.

Philidor's mate: *See* Smothered mate.

Piece: Although this can refer to any chess piece, it usually means a minor piece. "I just hung a piece" translates to: "I just left a Knight or Bishop *en prise.*"

Pin: A tactic by which one piece prevents another from moving, because doing so would either be illegal or create a discovery on another, more valued piece.

Ply: One half of a move pair, a single move for White or Black.

Positional: Concerned with a game's long-term effects, as opposed to *tactics.*

Postal chess: Chess by mail (a.k.a. correspondence chess).

Postmortem: The analysis that takes place after a game.

Pre-chess: A variation of chess in which the pieces are placed on the back ranks in any order the player chooses. Placing the pieces constitutes the first eight moves.

Provisional rating: An unofficial estimated rating based on the results of less than 20 tournament games.

Pup: Slang for perpetual check (a.k.a. "perp").

Queen: The most powerful chess piece, combining the powers of Rook and Bishop. A Queen may move any number of squares forward, backward, vertically, horizontally, or diagonally.

Quick chess: Chess played at a time control slower than *blitz chess* but quicker than *action chess* (generally ten to fifteen minutes per player per game).

Rating: Earned from the USCF for participating in official tournaments. The four-digit numbering system is divided into categories every two hundred points: from Master (2200 and above) to Class E (below 1200).

Rank: A horizontal row of squares on a chessboard (numbered 1 through 8).

Roll: A sequence of alternating checks by two pieces of like power which drive the enemy King to an edge or a corner (a.k.a. lawnmower technique).

Rook: The less valuable of the two major pieces. A Rook moves in a straight line any number of squares in any direction.

Rule of the square: A helpful analytical tool to determine quickly whether a lone King can catch an enemy passed pawn.

Sacrifice: The giving up of material for a future gain which (you hope) will more than compensate for the lost material.

Sandbagger: An inconsiderate, dishonest, and unethical player who deliberately loses games in order to lower his/her rating, so that he/she might later win money in a lower section of a big tournament.

Scholar's mate: Mate delivered when the Queen, supported by the King's Bishop, captures the pawn of f7 or f2, depending on who's checkmating whom.

Semi-open game: A game that starts 1. e2-e4, and is answered with a move other than 1. ... e7-e5 (a.k.a. half-open game).

Shot: An opportunity to execute a combination or a single move that will improve your position: "I missed a shot on move 17 and lost."

Simul: Shortened way of saying simultaneous exhibition (one player playing against several opponents at once).

Skewer: A tactic involving a Queen or Bishop aimed at more than one piece on the same rank, file or diagonal, so that one piece must fall (think *shish kebab!*).

Slow chess: Another name for traditional chess, often played at a time control of thirty moves in ninety minutes, followed by *sudden death.*

Smothered mate: A checkmate in which the King is trapped on all sides by his own men and has no place to flee (a.k.a. Philidor's mate).

Stalemate: A position in which a player has no legal moves, but his King is not in check. This position is a draw.

Staunton design: The standard design of chess pieces used today.

Strategy: Positional planning, general thinking; the opposite of *tactics*.

Sudden death: A time control in which the players have a set time to finish the game, no matter how many moves are involved.

Tactics: Specific combinations available in a given position; the opposite of *strategy*.

3D chess: Chess played on a three-tiered board—as if traditional chess weren't confusing enough.

TD: Tournament Director.

Tiebreaks: In the event of a tied score, a system used for deciding who wins a prize that cannot be split, such as a trophy.

Time control: A designated time allowance for a certain number of moves.

TN: Theoretical novelty; an opening move that is unfamiliar to analysts, but looks pretty good.

Touch-move: A rule requiring you to move the piece you've touched, if a legal move exists for that piece.

Unclear: A positional evaluation by grandmasters who don't feel like analyzing any further!

Universal notation: A method of recording moves in which pieces are designated by an actual picture of the piece itself, followed by the algebraic name for the square.

USCF: The U.S. Chess Federation.

WBCA: World Blitz Chess Association (the brainchild of Grandmaster Walter Browne).

Windmill attack: A combination in which a piece captures several enemy pieces via repeated discoveries on (usually) the King, which can only helplessly toggle back and forth as his army crumbles, piece by piece. (Usually involves a Rook on the seventh rank supported by a Bishop.)

Woodpusher: Slang for any chess player, but sometimes used to refer to a very weak chess player.

x: the symbol meaning "captures" or "takes."

Zugzwang: A pathetic state of affairs in which it's your move, but every move loses. In German, literally, "obligation to move."

Zwischenzug: German word for an in-between move, or a bit of finesse before continuing with an obvious sequence of moves.

The line between serious and spurious scholarship is an easy one to blur, with jargon on your side.
—David Lehman, "Archie Debunking" (1991).

When you are lonely, when you feel yourself an alien in the world, play chess. This will raise your spirits and be your counselor in war.

–Aristotle

CHAPTER TWELVE

How to Connect to the Whole World of Chess

Discovering chess is a wonderful moment in your life. Discovering how to get in touch with other people who love the game, and with clubs and even a national chess organization that exists to help you enjoy chess more, is a gratifying moment indeed, and one that used to depend mainly on good luck. But you live in an age where it is easier to find chess partners than at any other time in the history of the world.

Let's begin with how to contact humans. Chess offers you the opportunity to meet some fascinating people, and the chess community is the most accepting and egalitarian society you can ever find. Regardless of the kind of chess or chess event you're interested in, the place to start is clear.

The United States and the World Chess Federations

The official governing body of chess for the United States is the non-profit U.S. Chess Federation. Currently USCF has over 80,000 members and more than 2,000 officially affiliated clubs across the country. USCF or its affiliates organize all the official tournaments held in the U.S. They can be reached at: 3054 NYS Route 9W, New Windsor, NY 12553, Telephone: 800-388-KING (5464). USCF publishes *Chess Life*, the official journal of record of American chess.

And here's how to contact the World Chess Federation, or FIDE (Fédération Internationale des Échecs; the acronym is pronounced FEE-day): P.O. Box 166, CH-1000, Lausanne, 4, Switzerland. Telephone: 41 (21) 31 03 900. FIDE can provide contact information for any of more than 100 national chess federations worldwide.

The club scene

To get connected to the human side of chess, visit chess clubs. They range from school classrooms to multi-storied buildings with chess library rooms and tournament halls. Some of the fondest memories your authors have of our early days in chess are from the clubs–the games, the conversations, the characters and the lifelong friends. Clubs are the mother's lap of beginning chess players, and the extended family of the rest. Go there if you possibly can. Your national chess federation will tell you how to find one in your area.

Your regional association—and its publication

The most direct way to speak with a local chess voice is to contact your regional (state, province) association, the official representative of your national federation. No one knows the chess clubs and other opportunities in your home state or province better. Normally, each has its own publication. Subscribe! It's cheap, and it's filled with local names, events and news–pure fun for the chesser. Find out about your regional association from your national or world federation.

Tournaments

Chess tournaments are generally open to all–as spectators and participants. You should spend some time in the clubs, if you possibly can, before playing in your first tournament. You'll be a lot more comfortable with the customs, and you'll know some people.

Open tournaments are generally held on weekends, or as a club event on one or a series of evenings. Many offer *class prizes*. This means that you don't have to win the whole tournament, just do the best in your peer group to win a trophy or even some money. *Time controls*, the rules within a given tournament governing how quickly players must move, have speeded up greatly since the days of the cobwebs-between-chess-players cartoons. There's quite a range of "speed limits" now. A chess tournament no longer has to take your whole weekend!

Face-to-face (called *over-the-board,* or *OTB,* tournaments) are easy to find out about. Remember that number for the USCF? Call them, toll-free, and ask for a current issue of *Chess Life* magazine. Tell them you read about USCF in this book, and that you are thinking about joining. When the magazine arrives, look near the back, in the "Tournament Life" section. You'll see there are hundreds of tournaments every weekend, one probably very near you.

Chess through-the-mail

You can play chess without leaving your home, even without inviting someone over, in a number of ways. One way that's a lot of fun and very, very instructive is to play through the mail, normally sending postcards. This form of play is included in the term *correspondence chess* (which also includes chess by e-mail). It's also commonly called *postal chess*. You can meet chess players from all over. You can have a gaggle of games going at once. Postal players are sometimes zealously organized. Some carry on *hundreds* of games at the same time!

There are two particularly terrific organizations to contact to make playing correspondence chess easy. They'll assign your opponents, often in a special tournament that offers prizes. And should a dispute of some sort arise, they'll arbitrate. Every serious contest needs a referee!

✓ U.S. Chess Federation (picking up a pattern here?). Contact information above.

✓ American Postal Chess Tournaments (APCT). APCT also offers a bulletin on postal play, the *APCT News Bulletin*. Write to APCT at P.O. Box 305, Western Springs, Illinois, 60558; call them at (630) 663-0688; or e-mail them at APCT@AOL.com. APCT is run by Helen and Jim Warren, who have been friends to chess players and to organized chess for more decades than it's polite to discuss. They're dedicated to helping you enjoy your chess to the fullest. Jim is also a great person to call about any chess book you'd like to have—new or out of print.

Chess camps

Yes. Youngsters go to summer chess camps. Just as in a camp for any other discipline, top practitioners and teachers interact with the youngsters in a way that's impossible in a less playful, more time-restrained setting. Camps are a terrific way for kids to have a great time and improve their chess—as well as all those related thinking skills—in a few weeks.

By the way, teachers and parents rave about what chess has done to help their kids in school. Logic, focus and self-reliance are valuable attributes in every pursuit. The U.S. Chess Federation has information available on controlled studies showing that chess makes you smart. It can also send you lists of chess camps around the country.

Chess columns

Syndicated chess columns run in certain large-city papers or may appear in your local newspaper. Look for them or check with your national chess federation for a list.

Chess surfin'

If you have a PC with a connection to the Internet, or have access to one, you have chess on a technological platter. The web's always changing, of course, but the sites I'll mention are very well established. And the beauty of good web sites is that they generally offer automatic *links* with many other sites on the same subject. There are even sites that are nothing but long lists of *links* to other chess web sites. So your free "library" grows exponentially with each visit to a new site. Here are some of our favorites. The newsgroups given at the end of this chapter give anyone with an opinion and a keyboard a chance to post his thoughts to the world. Reviewing these is much like surfing your television's channels in the wee hours—you see some strange things!

www.chesscafe.com

Pure delight and diversity in everything chess! Here are: weekly book reviews, interactive bulletin board, end-game studies, chess links, classified ads, articles of both general and technical interest by the leading chess thinkers, photos, and much more. Updated frequently, so it's fun to visit often. This site even links to many foreign-language web sites. Want to practice your Hungarian while reading about chess? The Chess Cafe can take you there too. No fees.

www.chessclub.com

This is the site for the Internet Chess Club, which has been featured on America Online. Here the menu is on-line play! Although there is a modest annual fee to become a member, you can visit for a week at no charge. You see a chessboard on your screen, and move pieces with your mouse. As you win and lose games, you get a rating.  There's a dialog window that lets you chat with your opponent, or with groups of hundreds of other chess players, worldwide, who are on line at that moment. On a given evening you can play and chat with chess buddies from Hong Kong, Sweden, Spain, Germany, South Africa, New Zealand, as well as the U.S. You can play chess computer programs here as well! Test out the tips in this book—even at three A.M. (it's daytime or early evening somewhere)!

www.tcc.net/twic/twic.html

Known commonly as "TWIC," is This Week in Chess. Here, you can catch up on what's happened in chess each week, and find chess games from many national and international events.

www.uschess.org

The official home page of the U.S. Chess Federation. Lots of information about the organization, good links, and a very easy way for anyone surfing the web to contact USCF about anything.

Newsgroups (Usenet)

rec.games.chess.analysis
rec.games.chess.computer
rec.games.chess.misc
rec.games.chess.play-by-email
rec.games.chess.politics

The web's already full of chess action. And the technology and the medium are bound to get better and better.

The game of chess is the touchstone to the intellect.
—Goethe

USCF's Let's Play Chess*—A Quick Reference for Beginners

Summary of the moves of chess

Chess is a game for two players, one with "White" pieces and one with "Black" pieces. At the beginning of the game, the pieces are set up as pictured below. (See diagrams to identify pieces.) These hints will help you to remember the proper board setup:

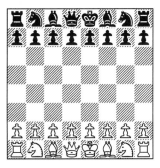

1. Opposing Kings and Queens go directly opposite each other.
2. The square in the lower right-hand corner is a light one ("light on right").
3. The White Queen goes on a light square, the Black Queen on a dark square ("Queen on color").

The pieces and how they move

White always moves first, and then the players take turns moving. Only one piece may be moved at each turn (except for "castling," a special move that is explained later). The Knight is the only piece that can jump over other pieces. All other pieces move only along unblocked lines. You may not move a piece to a square already occupied by one of your own pieces. But you can capture an enemy piece that stands on a square where one of your pieces can move. Simply remove the enemy piece from the board and put your own piece in its place.

The King The King is the most important piece. When he is trapped, his whole army loses. The King can move one square in any direction—for example, to any of the squares with dots in this diagram. (An exception is castling, which is explained later.) The King may never move into check—that is, onto a square attacked by an opponent's piece.

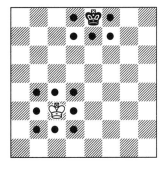

*Reprinted with the permission of the U.S. Chess Federation.

The Queen The Queen is the most powerful piece. She can move any number of squares in any direction—horizontal, vertical, or diagonal—if her path is not blocked. She can reach any of the squares with dots in the diagram at right.

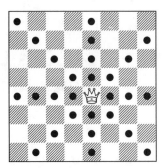

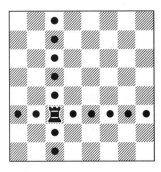

The Rook The Rook is the next-most powerful piece. It can move any number of squares vertically or horizontally, if its path is not blocked.

The Bishop The Bishop can move any number of squares diagonally if its path is not blocked. Note that this Bishop starts on a light square and can reach only other light squares. At the beginning of the game, you have one "dark-square" Bishop and one "light-square" Bishop.

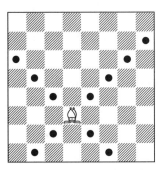

The Knight The Knight's move is special. It hops directly from its old square to its new square. The Knight can jump over other pieces between its old and new squares. Think of the Knight's move as an "L." It moves two squares horizontally or vertically and then makes a right-angle turn for one more square. The Knight always lands on a square opposite in color from its old square.

The pawn The pawn moves straight ahead (never backwards), but it captures diagonally. It moves one square at a time, but on its first move it has the option of moving forward one or two squares. In the diagram (see page 139), the squares with dots indicate possible destinations for the pawns. The White pawn is on its original square, so it may move ahead either one or two squares. The Black pawn has already moved, so it may move ahead only one square at a time. The squares on which these pawns may capture are indicated by an X. If a pawn advances all the way to the opposite end of the board, it is immediately "promoted" to another piece, usually a Queen. It may not remain a pawn or become a King. Therefore, it is possible for each player to have more than one Queen or more than two Rooks, Bishops, or Knights on the board at the same time.

Special moves

Castling Each player may "castle" only once during a game and when conditions are met. Castling is a special move that lets a player move two pieces at once: the King and one Rook. In castling, the player moves his King two squares to its left or right toward one of his Rooks. At the same time, the Rook involved goes to the square beside the King and toward the center of the board (see illustrations below). In order to castle, neither the King nor the Rook involved may have moved before. Also, the King may not castle out of check, into check, or through check. Further, there may not be pieces of either color between the King and the Rook involved in castling. Castling is often a very important move because it allows you to place your King in a safe location and also allows the Rook to become more active. When the move is legal, each player has the choice of castling *kingside* or *queenside* or not at all—no matter what the other player chooses to do.

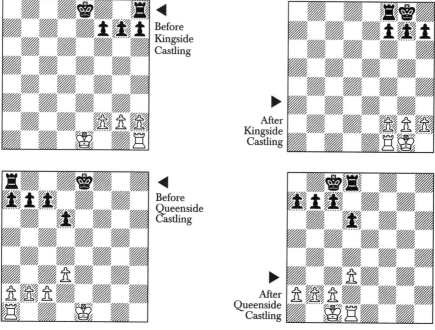

Before Kingside Castling

After Kingside Castling

Before Queenside Castling

After Queenside Castling

En passant This French phrase is used for a special pawn capture. It means "in passing," and it occurs when one player moves a pawn two squares forward to try to avoid capture by the opponent's pawn. The capture is made exactly as if the player had moved the pawn only one square forward. In the diagram at right, the Black pawn moves up two squares to the square with the dot. On its turn the White pawn may capture the Black one on the square marked with the X. If the White player does not exercise this option immediately—before playing some other move—the Black pawn is safe from "en passant" capture for the rest of the game. But new opportunities may arise for each pawn in similar circumstances.

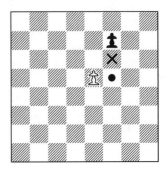

About check and checkmate

The main goal of chess is to checkmate your opponent's King. The King is not actually captured and removed from the board like other pieces. But if the King is attacked ("checked") and threatened with capture, it must get out of check immediately. If there is no way to get out of check, the position is a "checkmate," and the side that is checkmated loses. You may not move into check: For example, moving into a direct line with your opponent's Rook, if there are no other pieces between the Rook and your King, is not a legal move. Otherwise, the Rook could "capture" the King, which is not allowed. If you are in check, there are three ways of getting out:

1. Capturing the attacking piece
2. Placing one of your own pieces between the attacker and your King (unless the attacker is a Knight)
3. Moving the King away from the attack

If a checked player can do none of these, he is checkmated and loses the game. If a King is not in check, but that player can make no legal move, the position is called a *stalemate* and the game is scored as a *draw*, or tie.

Index

About the Authors

AL LAWRENCE was Executive Director of the U. S. Chess Federation during a decade of record-breaking growth. A former public school and college teacher with advanced degrees in instructional techniques, he is especially interested in applying modern teaching theory to chess instruction. He is president of OutExcel!, a marketing and management consulting firm, writes widely on chess, and serves as adviser to a leading chess computer manufacturer. His interests range from Chaucer to martial arts. He lives in the Village of Wallkill, 70 miles north of New York City.

GRANDMASTER LEV ALBURT is a former two-time European Cup Chess Champion, three-time Ukrainian Champion, two-time U.S. Open Champion, and three-time U.S. Invitational Champion. He was born in Orenburgh, Russia. He taught chess in the Soviet Union under the tutelage of the eminent teacher and three-time World Chess Champion Mikhail Botvinnik. In 1979, while in West Germany taking part in an international chess tournament, he defected. GM Alburt, a renowned teacher, is author and publisher of the best-selling, six-volume *Comprehensive Chess Course*, based on formerly secret Soviet lesson plans. He lives in New York City.

A free offer!

Exclusively for this book, USCF is offering, at no charge, to mail anyone in the U.S. a very informative, 16-page booklet entitled "Basic Chess Curriculum." Write or call the USCF (Dept. 70) at:

    USCF (Dept. 70)
    3054 NYS Route 9W
    New Windsor, NY 12553
    Telephone: 800-388-KING (5464)